BOOKS BY DANIEL HOFFMAN

POETRY

Brotherly Love
The Center of Attention
Broken Laws
Striking the Stones
The City of Satisfactions
A Little Geste
An Armada of Thirty Whales

PROSE

Poe Poe Poe Poe Poe Poe Poe
Barbarous Knowledge
Form and Fable in American Fiction
The Poetry of Stephen Crane
Paul Bunyan, Last of the Frontier Demigods

AS EDITOR

Harvard Guide to Contemporary American Writing
American Poetry and Poetics

BROTHERLY LOVE

DANIEL HOFFMAN

BROTHERLY LOVE

The wolf did with the lambkin dwell in peace,
His grim carniv'rous nature there did cease;

When the great P E N N his famous treaty made
With indian chiefs beneath the Elm tree's shade.

    —EDWARD HICKS

America is a poem in our eyes.

    —EMERSON, 'THE POET'

VINTAGE BOOKS
A Division of Random House · New York

FIRST VINTAGE BOOKS EDITION MARCH 1981

Sections 31–35 and 37–39 have originally appeared in
The Hudson Review. Section 60 originally appeared in
The Georgia Review. Sections 1, 3, 11 and 61 are
reprinted with revisions from *Striking the Stones*, and
Section 34 from *Broken Laws*, by Daniel Hoffman.

Library of Congress Cataloging in Publication Data
Hoffman, Daniel, 1923-
Brotherly love.
1. Penn, William, 1644-1718—Poetry. I. Title.
PS3515.02416B74 1981b   811'.54   80-54229
ISBN 0-394-74726-7

FOR ROBERT PENN WARREN

I take history
to represent us
as in a glass

or as if the dead were returned

to report to us
the actions done
in their time;

it is a sort of pre-existence

making us
to have always lived
or to have lived

and had knowledge before we were born.

— WILLIAM PENN

CONTENTS

I

TREATING WITH INDIANS

Facts yield their secret sense
and poetry and annals are alike.

—EMERSON, 'HISTORY'

I

Smudge from a balky lighter
and a low-hulled, smoking tramp
blurs the docks. Down Market Street
the fierce moonlight of mercury lamps

sanitizes pavements Walt
Whitman used to walk.
Here Poe and Brockden Brown
were stalked by demons through the town

past the dormered brickwork houses
of our Colonial century
(now lavishly restored
to Federal austerity)

where shoppers jostle. Wait! I'd join
you, seers of the soul's exile!
From Christ Church vaults the pigeons foul
our Signers seem to give no sign,

but over Wanamaker's lights
Billy Penn extends indulgent arms,
still beckoning the Welsh and Mennonites
to his green outlying farms . . .

2

If there is a spirit of this place,

if these heights sloping downward to the riverbank,
these hills furrowed by creeks that furl and ripple
through the turning valleys
burbling
into one another,

pouring their darkly silted waters stained with Autumn leaves,
their froths of melted snow or waterwalls
the furious runoffs
of Spring rains
into the river,

if these woods and meadows, thickety fields and marshes,
no matter now
how deeply hacked and torn, dug out,
uprooted, bulldozed,
levelled and built over,

have a spirit of their own,

if we can believe
in ghosts that walk here where these sands and soils
and stones once felt
their living tread,

their deeds linger as a fragrance
in the burning leaves or the sting
of sleet upon the forehead
lingers,

a presence of the Indian Pipe in forest compost
or Blackburnian warbler heard, unseen,
yet tinting with its trill or trembling shade
the air we breathe,

absorbed into our breath, our blood,
our selves,
an unseen hand laid on our consciences

in this place —

3

The emissaries they have sent us
From the tall country of the antlers
—Flint barbs fiercely glistening
And the light glinting on their feathered robes—

What brings them, grave and silent, to our study?
If they would show
The signs, if they'd spell on our ground
Those names the sun acknowledges . . .

What must we pledge to render unto them?

4

Do you think you choose
The shape from whose
Beak or mouth
You learn your truth?

5

From emptiness without center
From the blackness of the nowhere
Before the stars pitched their lodgepoles
From the bottom of the sky
From deep sea-muck

Beneath the earth came Turtle, Great
Grandfather, swimming
In the wrinkled shadows of my sleep,
Speaking
In my voice:

Is it real, this life
That you are living, is it
Real? Remember,
In the time of Hawk, of White Frog,
You knew how the world was made.

6

HOW THE WORLD WAS MADE

(A reconstruction of the *Walam Olum*, or *Red Score*, of the
Lenni Lenape, based upon their pictographs on maple shingles
and the words these served to recall, from the sole copy obtained
in 1820 by C. F. Rafinesque and by him transcribed.)

 1 Before the beginning and forever lasting,
      Sky and clouds
      Over the earth,

 2 Fog clung to the earth. There,
      Manito, the Wonder-Doer,
      Kept his home.

 3 Lost in space, before time was,
      When nothingness came, Manito
      Stayed everywhere.

 4 He made the four quarters of the earth,
      Rivers and the sea he made
      And land beyond the sea.

5 He made the moon, made elder brother sun
      And in the arching sky
      The stars, the grandfathers.

 6 He made the sun move and the stars
      Turn in their places, he made
      The twelve moons swell.

9

7 He made the wind blow with good deeds,
The sky cleared and the water
Touched with many ripples.

8 He made islands rise from under water,
And there, beneath the sky,
He remained.

9 Then again the Great Spirit, Manito,
He made the other spirits,
Manito to manitos.

10 Hidden in his mystery he made
All persons whose destiny is death
And souls for all of them.

11 And ever after on the earth he was
Manito to young men, to grown men
And their grandfathers.

12 He gave men the first
Mother of all persons
Protected from above.

13 In the sea he gave the fish and turtles
On water and on land, gave beasts,
And birds gave in the sky.

14 There was a Manito of evil made
15 Strong men and monsters in the water,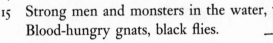
Blood-hungry gnats, black flies.

16 Earth, then, was the lodge all sat in,
Many peoples lived at peace,
Were friends.

17 Beneath the arch of heaven and sun
With the hallowed Lenape
The Manito remained.

18 In those days the Spirit sent
The first young men after the women,
The first mothers,

19 Who went to gather their first food
The berries, and the young men
Followed after.

20 In those days all knew contentedness.
Life was easy then on earth, living
Was pleasure.

21 But under the earth, in secret came
The power of the snake, a shaman's helper
Bringing evil.

22 Brought meanness with him,
Destruction came then, and black deeds
Came there.

23 Storm clouds came, starvation came.
Killing came. He brought death.
Evil, evil, evil.

24 All the people from across the water,
The great villages of the first land
Of the twin turtles Truth and Falseness,
There they remained.

(Here follows the story of the flood and the history of
the Lenni Lenape, their wars and their wanderings.)

```
 ↓ 7
```

[Canto V]

1   Long ago,
    There, in the distant land of pines
    The Talega country
    They lived at peace.

2   In that time
    Road-Man was chief
    There, in the middle reaches
    Of Wapanaleng River.

3   In the days
    When White Lynx was chief
    They planted corn,
    Harvested much.

4   There were many
    People in the time
    When the chief was He-Who-Dreams-
    Of-Good-Things.

5   In the time
    When He-Who-Writes was chief
    With red paint on maple shingles
    They fixed the true.

·   ·   ·   ·   ·

51   In the time
When He-Who-Lives-Yonder
Was chief they pitched their wigwams
At the water's edge.

52a Then they did
What they desired—the one tribe parted
Into clans: the Turtle, Wolf,
And Turkey totems,

52b Each one followed
Customs of their own
As they had done
Since the beginning.

53   In the time
When He-Who-Fails-at-Water's-Edge
Was chief they ravaged
The Senecas' possessions.

54   In the time
When Friendly One was chief
He played his games of war
With the Senecas.

55   In the time
When He-Who-Greets-Others
Was chief, some of the tribe
Went yonder,

56   Crossing the waters
Of the Scioto River
Among the enemy tribe
Whom they hated.

57 When White Frog
Was chief, at that time
His people lived
Along the sea.

58 In the time
When Hawk was chief
They were looking, looking
Out on the water.

59 At this time
Floating on the ocean
From the north, from the south
The white men came—

60 They are peaceful,
They are friendly, bringing
Great possessions, a strange tongue.
Who are they?

(Here ends the *Walam Olum*)

8

Ripples of the tidal river
Break with feathery touch among the reeds,

Waves that rolled across the shifting ocean
From the shores of Cornwall, rolling westward.

The cattails in the mudflats wafted
From Siberia, the feathery seedpods tumbling

From pond and stream across a continent.
The Lenape came on a trail of rushes,

A dozen dozen generations following
The promise of the rising sun and moon.

Toward setting suns the English pointed prows,
Toward moons that sink each morning in the sea.

Where ripples break against the swaying rush-stems
The destinations of two journeys meet.

Behind the clouds an unseen witness—
Great Manito, the Lord, whose will is done.

9

Everything so far results from the motion of irresistible forces.
  History is what has happened, nor is it hospitable to
  questions the event proves irrelevant: What if . . . ?
  Supposing. . . . What is given is all that is given; we,
  coming afterward, have no choice in the matter.

The past, then, lies upon the present like a giant's dead body.
  Or is it a cast-iron railway coach of obsolete design in
  which we clatter down rigid rails that stretch backward
  further than eyes can see? We have come careening on that
  road, our antiquated equipment screeching sparks at every
  turn as we rush precipitately toward a future we can neither
  see nor conceive . . .

But what was it like, then, when a moment of this past that now
  constrains us between iron rails was itself the present, riding
  inexorably down the rigid track of an elder past prior to
  itself? Didn't its participants live out their predetermined
  choices supposing it was they who actually chose their
  destinies?

     To the Emperor of Canada,

Penn's letter to the Chief Sachem of the Lenni Lenape began,
  the Proprietor mistaking the geography of the King of
  England's patent, or else supposing that the naked savage he
  would treat with owned not five miles of meadows but a
  continent entire,

       The Great God
            that made thee and me
               and all the World

Incline our hearts
    to love peace and Justice
        that we may live

Friendly together
    as becomes the workmanship
        of the great God.

Lord, Lord, what Christian speaks thus to the Salvage Man,
    when northward, in the Colonies it pleases Thee to plant
    deep in this heathen wilderness, May apple and bunchberry
    freshly cover charred stockade, the bloodied campfires, the
    abandoned graves,

King Philip's body drawn and quartered, his head splayed on a
    pole at Plymouth, his Narragansetts slain, their squaws and
    children hacked inside the wigwam, and the forest strewn
    with English soldiers' buttons, buckles, and the bones of
    corpses whose scalp-locks dangled from the waists of braves
    the musket-ball cut down;

The King of England
    who is a great Prince
        hath for divers Reasons

Granted to me
    a large Country
        in America

Which however I
    am willing to Injoy
        upon friendly termes with thee.

Ever present though invisible, in the blue haze of their campfire,
    Clio, known to the Lenape by whatever name, hovers in the
    air, if not by foreknowledge burdened then astonished to
    behold

After half a century of treachery and murder, ambush, deadly
   fires, over treaties sworn but broken, over stolen land, these
   so different races, faiths, these polities with knowledge and
   expectations never yet once reconciled confront each other,
   saying,

>   And this I will say
>   that the people who come with me
>   are a just plain and honest people
>
>   that neither make war upon others
>   nor fear war from others
>   because they will be just.

A peculiar people, these, for a King, for whatever divers
   Reasons, to grant a large Country . . . How came he to give
   it them, why came they here, and why their Penn was
   mightier than the sword, these words of mine and his
   explore.

These words I offer her, who hovers, astonished still, above,
   around, and after the doing of these deeds and the hearing
   of their telling, she who has received so many Epics, so
   many noble Histories, so many Heroic Songs,

>   I have sett up
>   a Society of Traders
>   in my Province
>
>   to traffick with thee
>   and thy people
>   for your Commodities
>
>   that you may be furnished
>   with that which is good
>   at reasonable rates.

—Heroic Songs of Commerce and Good Trade! Will she accept
　　these lays, so used to martial airs and funeral odes, to battle
　　cries and shows of valor,

How will she take these strophes framed with prudent
　　calculation by the Leader of a people honest, just and plain?

Ah, Muse of sterner songs, frown not upon my lines, but listen
　　while the Founder of the Heavenly City here on Earth,
　　who is in the World as well as Heaven, says,

　　　　I have already taken Care
　　　　　　that none of my people wrong you
　　　　　　　　by good laws I have provided

　　　　for that purpose . . .
　　　　　　if anything should be
　　　　　　　　out of order,

　　　　expect when I come
　　　　　　it shall be mended,
　　　　　　　　and I will bring you

　　　　some things of our Country
　　　　　　that are useful
　　　　　　　　and pleasing to you.

　　　　So rest in ye Love
　　　　　　of our god y^t made us
　　　　　　　　I am

　　　　Your Loveing Friend

　　　　　　　　　　　　　　　Wm. Penn

　1 6 8 2 .

10

Not the shrill flageolet and snare, the clank of armor and
    whipping snaffle of the wind

As pennants break out and snap above the glints of sun on
    breastplate,

Not the silence brooding in the woods, the simulated whistle of
    the mourning-dove

Roo-cooing from the fallen log, the thicket overlooking steep
    defiles

As scouts, as quietly as shadows among wavering sunbeams,
    squint through clefts in foliage,

Not the commanded shout, the clackety rattle of priming-rods in
    gunsnouts or the click of hammers cocked

Nor the inaudible tension as the arrow rests on thumbcrotch and
    the drawn thong tautens,

None of these the sounds or silences that day, as Englishmen
    and Lenni Lenape

Gather and palaver on the river's edge, learning each others'
    words and gestures,

Acknowledging the signs, repeating names

The sun makes manifest that men can trust in.

II

This life we are living,
Is it real? Is it
Here that glory is,

Or in the Life immortal?
The Lord Who works His will
In this world, on our souls

Has set His Seal of Love.
His Seal is on the souls
Of all men, even these

Ignorant of Christ,
Naked, in flints and feathers,
Yet Children of the Seed.

This Life our brothers lead
—How strange to us!—the Lord
As He gives ours, gives them:

12

'They are generally tall, straight, well-built, and of singular
    Proportion;
they tread strong and clever, and mostly walk with lofty Chin:
of Complexion, Black, but by design, as the Gypsies in England:
They grease themselves with Bears-fat clarified, and using no
    defense
against Sun or Weather, their skins must needs be swarthy;
Their Eye is little and black, not unlike a straight-look't Jew.
The thick Lip and flat Nose, so frequent with the East-Indians
    and Blacks, are not common to them;
for I have seen as comely European-like faces among them of
    both, as on your side the Sea;
and truly an Italian Complexion hath not much more of the
    White,
and the Noses of several of them have as much of the Roman.

13

'For their Original, I am ready to believe them
of the Jewish Race,
I mean, of the stock of the Ten Tribes,
and that for the following Reasons; first,
They were to go to a Land not planted or known, which to be
     sure Asia and Africa were, if not Europe;
and he that intended that extraordinary Judgment upon them,
might make the Passage not uneasie to them,
as it is not impossible in it self,
from the Easter-most parts of Asia,
to the Wester-most of America.

'In the next place, I find them of like Countenance
and their Children of so lively Resemblance,
that a man would think himself in Dukes-place or Berry-street in
     London, when he seeth them.

'But this is not all, they agree in Rites,
they reckon by Moons:
they offer their first Fruits,
they have a kind of Feast of Tabernacles;
they are said to lay their Altar upon twelve Stones;
their Mourning a year, Customs of Women, with many things
     that do not now occur.

'Their Language is lofty, yet narrow, but like the Hebrew;
in Signification full, like Short-hand in writing; one
Word
serveth in the place of three, and the rest are supplied
by the Understanding of the Hearer;

I have made it my business
to understand it, that I might not want an Interpreter on any
    occasion. And I must say,
that I know not a Language spoken in Europe, that hath words
of more sweetness or greatness, in Accent and Emphasis,
than theirs; for Instance,
    Octorockon,
            Rancocas,
                    Oricton,
                            Shakamaxon,
                                    Poquessin,
all of which are names of Places,
and have Grandeur in them:
Of words of Sweetness,
Anna is Mother,
                Issimus, a Brother,
                            Netap, Friend,
usque oret, very good;
                    pone, Bread,
                            metse, eat,
matta, no,
            hatta, to have,
                    payo, to come;

Sepassen, Passion, the Names of Places; *Tamany, Siccane,*
    Sectareus, are names of Persons.
If one asks them for anything they have not, they will answer,
mattá ne hattá,
which to translate is, not I have, instead of I have not.

15

'They care for little, because they want but little;
and the Reason is,
a little contents them:
In this
they are sufficiently revenged on us;
if they are ignorant of our Pleasures, they are also free from
    our Pains.
They are not disquieted with Bills of Lading and Exchange,
nor perplexed with Chancery-Suits and
    Exchequer-Reckonings.
We sweat and toil to live;
their pleasure feeds them,
I mean, their Hunting, Fishing and Fowling,
and this Table is spread every where;
they eat twice a day, Morning and Evening:
their Seats and Table are the Ground.

16

'These poor People are under a dark Night
in things relating to Religion,
yet they believe in God
and Immortality,
without the help of Metaphysicks; for they say,
There is a great King that made them,
who dwells in a glorious Country to the Southward of
    them,
and that the Souls of the good shall go thither,
where they shall live again.

17

'Their Worship consists of two parts.
Their Sacrifice is their first Fruits;
the first and fattest Buck they kill, goeth to the fire,
where he is all burnt with a Mournful Ditty of him that
      performeth the Ceremony,
but with such marvelous Fervency and Labour of Body,
that he will even sweat to a foam.

'The other part is their *Cantico,* performed by
      round-Dances,
sometimes Words,
sometimes Songs,
then Shouts,
two being in the middle that begin, and by Singing
and Drumming on a Board direct the Chorus:
Their Postures in the Dance are very Antick and differing,
but all keep measure.
This is done with equal Earnestness and Labour,
but great appearance of Joy.

❦ 18

'In the Fall, when the Corn cometh in,
they begin to feast one another;
there have been two great Festivals already, to which all
    come that will:
I was at one myself;
their Entertainment
was a green Seat by a Spring,
under some shady Trees,
and twenty Bucks, with hot Cakes of new Corn, both
    Wheat and Beans,
which they make up in a square form, in the leaves of the
    Stem,
and bake them in Ashes.
And after that they fell to Dance,
But they that go, must carry
a small Present in their Money,
it may be six Pence,
which is made of the Bone of a Fish;
the black is with them as Gold, the white, Silver;
they call it *Wampum*.

19

'Their Government is by Kings,
which they call *Sachema*, and those by Succession,
but always of the Mothers side; for Instance,
the Children of him that is now King, will not succeed,
but his Brother by the Mother, or the Children of his
 Sister, whose Sons (and after them the Children
 of her Daughters)
will reign; for no Woman inherits;
the Reason they render for this way of Descent is,
that their Issue may not be spurious.

'Every King hath his Council,
of all the Old and Wise men of his Nation,
 which perhaps is two hundred People;
nothing of Moment is undertaken,
be it War, Peace, Selling of Land or Traffick,
without advising with them; and which is more,
with the Young Men too.
'Tis admirable to consider,
how Powerful the Kings are, and yet how they move
by the Breath of their People.

'I have had occasion to be in Council with them upon
    Treaties for Land, and to adjust the terms of Trade;
their Order is thus:
The King
sits in the middle of an half Moon,
and hath his Council, the Old and Wise on each hand;
behind them, or at a little distance, sit the younger Fry, in
    the same figure.
Having consulted and resolved their business, the King
    ordered one of them to speak to me;
he stood up, came to me, and in the Name of his King
    saluted me,
then took me by the hand,
and told me, That he was ordered by his King
to speak to me, and that now it was not he, but the King
    that spoke,
because what he should say, was the King's mind.
'Having thus introduced his matter, he fell to the Bounds of
    the Land
and the Price
(which now is little and dear, that which would have
    bought twenty Miles, not buying now two).
During the time this Person spoke, not a man of them was
    observed
to whisper or smile; the Old, Grave, the Young, Reverend
    in their Deportment;
they do speak little, but fervently, and with Elegancy:
I have never seen more natural Sagacity,

considering them without the help (I was agoing to say, the
      spoil) of Tradition;
and he will deserve the Name of Wise,
that outwits them
in any Treaty about a thing they understand.'

21

INSTRUCTIONS TO A PAINTER

For the Drawing of the Posture and Progress of the
Proprietor's Treaty with the Indians at Shakamaxon
on the Delaware, in 1 6 8 2.

Let History provide its Theme—
    The noblest action of the race.
A State is founded on the dream
    Thy hand shall draft, thy brush retrace;

Recall that Faith, known as a boy,
    When Friends met in thy Father's home;
The Silence; Inward Light; then Joy.
    A greater power than raised up Rome

Drew here the great Proprietor,
    With Love, and Justice, in his heart.
On childhood's scenes, recalled, outpour
    This consummation of thy art:

In the right foreground, an Indian dame
    Gives her swaddling babe the breast,
Each wholly innocent of shame;
    That child's, the *Future,* which is bless'd.

With natural grace the Lenape
    Are grouped as though sprung from the Land;
The Quakers, stiffly, garbed in gray,
    Before their new-built houses stand.

Beneath the Shackamaxon elm
    He smiles, and graciously extends
The liberal hand that guides the realm
    To his trusting Savage friends.

A dozen Sachems gather round;
    In chieftain's hand, the Peace-Pipe rests.
Two seamen, kneeling on the ground,
    Show linens to Penn's naked guests.

At the left, some kilted sailors sit
    While another carries from the shore
A crate with the Old World's wealth in it.
    The Sachems pow-wow, asking more.

Thy paints shall celebrate what Penn
    Wrought with those Indians in the glade:
No wars nor warpaints mar these men
    Whom God in His own Image made.

Friend Benjamin, thee has done well indeed, thy native genius
and laborious skill making this image the world cannot
forget,

Thy vision of the scene, a century later than the action, making
of the scene a vision, as my words would re-enact it two
centuries after thee,

The truth of Fact being great but greater still the visionary truth
of Art, else how could we but demur

That the portly Penn you picture was in truth but thirty-eight
and in his prime, nor did the Friends appear

As on the Quaker Oats box, in broad-brimmed hats and dun
frock-coats like those thy father wore,

Till half a century after Penn, nor was the site adorned with
triple-decker mansions built of brick just then,

When squat log cabins were all there was of Philadelphia;

Nor do we mind that the stout fellow in your painting near to
Penn is in fact your father Mr. West,

While your brother Thomas leans there on a cane, or that
recorded history cannot show

A treaty ever made at Shackamaxon in the elm tree's shade—

No matter, it was for this thee in thy boyhood, out of thy
father's sight,

Made paint brush from tufts of a squirrel's tail tied to a twig and
dipped in the juices

Thee squeezed from nuts and fruits—the Indians showed thee
how—and dabbled on a fresh-cut board

Thy worldly images, inimical to the upright puritanic Friends,

Who yet, thy talent persevering against disapprobation, at last considered, and agreed

That a lad may be an artist and a Quaker too, and sent thee off to study far from them,

Thee never returning home from London, where the Delaware at Shackamaxon flowed

Through thy imagination when Mr. Thomas Penn requested thee,

The Fellow of the Royal Academy and Painter to King George,

To memorialize his father, and thy subject became clarified in mind,

Although within five years thee would be in exile from a country, not a colony, where war

Would stain and scar the woods and villages that thee dearly remembered,

And new plaques in memory of English youths be affixed to walls of parish churches,

The sufferings, the griefs of war making more precious thoughts and images

Of peace and the great Peace-Maker, the image thee devised

Admired by many and desired by all, both art and industry combining

To bring in sundry forms to many folk the simulacra of thy vision—

Printed on linen fabrics, made into curtains, valences, and bedspreads such

As the quilt handsewn by Martha Washington beneath which slept

The Father of His Country, inheritor of Penn's title, First in
     Peace,

Copies of 'Penn's Treaty with the Indians' appearing
     subsequently

On dishes, platters, cups, and bowls of China-ware, the buildings

Of early Philadelphia now pagodas, the elm-trees, palms,

While these details resemble yours more closely on luminescent
     candle-screens

And shimmering lampshades in white Parian-ware,

Or stand blunt and crudely rendered in hand-blown glass, tin
     trays, and cast-iron stoves,

Or with finesse on linen tapestries and bronze medallions, while
     in 1838

A statuary tableau presented well-carved Indians, Quakers,
     sailors, mother and babe

In miniature at the Chester County Horticultural Society Fair,

William Penn at once discerned in his blue scarf, discerned
     perhaps

By those who'd stopped for a few in Russelville beneath the sign
     of the tavern called

'Penn's Treaty with the Indians,' the scene long since across the
     water copied, printed, sold

By Hall and Boydell, whose litho print of 1775 was a perfect
     transfer of the scene

Accurate in each detail—save that the picture is reversed,

This error being copied in many a later print, etching, painting,
     lithograph

In England, France, and Philadelphia, not counting J. Hoover
    whose large mezzotint

In 1862, with the nation yet again at war, showed, crudely, all

The figures where West placed them, Quakers left, Indians
    right,

But acknowledged in the midst of casualties the nation could
    scarcely bear

The sight of an Indian mother's naked bosom, so provided

Her suckling infant with her fingers, not her breast,

As may be seen now at the Inn at Marshalltown, Pa.,

In time of war West's original itself exhibited in Philadelphia, in
    Logan Square,

June 1864, in the William Penn Parlor of the Great Central Fair

Of the United States Sanitary Commission, precursor of Red
    Cross,

For the benefit of the wounded such as those Walt Whitman
    nursed,

The spirit of the Peace-Maker most strong when needed most,

The painting copied, reproduced, and by the century's end

Photographed and published in a dozen dozen magazines and
    books,

Always a rush of interest in the painting of Penn's Treaty

Whenever Penn's country is at war,

In 1941 Penn's Treaty on each card in decks of playing cards,

On Provident Insurance Company calendars and in the Bulletin
    of the Friends

Historical Association, in ads in *Newsweek, Time*

And full-color in encylopedias printed despite the shortages of
  war,

Since then, the country constantly at war, West's Treaty
  reappearing

In books on history, on painting, and on Benjamin West,

On Quakers, Pennsylvania, Christianity in the United States,

In *Our Heritage, Landmarks of Liberty, Corse di Storia*

E di Educazione Civica (in Rome), in books in Sweden,
  Germany, England of course, and France,

Made into slides for the National Gallery and the Metropolitan
  Museum,

Reproduced in *Kleine Schriften zu Kunst, Literatur, Philosophie,
  Geschichte und Politik,*

And *The American Heritage History of the United States,*

Shown on TV, the paintings of the painting and the copies

In litho or engraving, book or magazine

All collectible and valued at a price, some even beyond price,

West's original, for instance, long shown in Independence Hall,

Now at the Pennsylvania Academy of Fine Arts, where
  thousands see it,

Many sending an image of its image

On color postcards home—

But few, how few, of those who've pondered the Great
  Peace-Maker

And his stolid Quakers and the Indian chief and sachems

And the lithe-limbed Indian mother with her babe sucking her
  breast

Or fingers, how few have ever read or even wondered

What, exactly what, in truth, was promised and agreed to,

Deliberated and palavered, signed and the Peace-Pipe smoked on

—I mean the text, that tells who gave, who got

How much for what at Shackamaxon

In Penn's Treaty with the Indians?

𝖳𝗁𝗂𝗌 𝕴𝗇𝗱𝖾𝗇𝗍𝗎𝗋𝖾

made the fifteenth day of July in the yeare of o^r Lord
according to the English Accompt
one Thousand Six Hundred Eighty & Two

B E T W E E N E Idquahon, Janottowe Idqueqeywon Sahoppe
for himself & Okonickon,
Merkekowen, Oreckton for Nannacussey Shaurwaughon,
Swanpisse, Nahoosey,
Tomackhickon, Westkekitt & Tohawsiz
Indyan Sachamakers of one pte

And William Penn Esqr
Chiefe Proprieto^r of the Province of Pennsylvania
of the other pte

W I T N E S S E T H That for & in Consideracon
of the Sumes & pticulers of Goods,
Merchandizes, & Utensills herein after menconed & expressed
(That is to say)

Three Hundred & fifty ffathams of Wampum,
Twenty White Blankitts,
Twenty ffathams of Strawd waters,
Sixty ffathams of Duffields,
Twenty kettles ffower wherof large,

Twenty Gunns,
Twenty Coates,
fforty Shirts,
fforty payre of Stockings,

Fforty Howes,
fforty Axes,
Two Barrells of Powder,
Two Hundred Barres of Lead,

Two Hundred Knives,
Two Hundred Small Glasses,
Twelve paire of Shooes,

fforty Copper Boxes,
fforty Tobacco Tongs,
Two small Barrells of Pipes,
fforty paire of Sissers,
fforty Combes
Twenty fower pounds of Red Lead,
one Hundred Aules,
Two handfulls of fish hooks,

Two handfulls of needles,
fforty pounds of Shott,
Tenne Bundles of Beades,

Tenne Small Sawes,
Twelve drawing knives,
ffower Anchors of Tobacco,
Two Anchors of Rumme,
Two Anchors of Syder,
Two Anchors of Beere
and Three Hundred Gilders by the said William Penn

His Agents or Assignes to the Said
Indyan Sachamakers for the use
of them & their People
at & before
Sealleing & Delivery
hereof in hand paid & Delivered
whereof & whewith they the Said Sachamakers

doe hereby acknowledge themselves fully Satisfyed
Contented & paid

The Said Indyan Sachamakers (ptys to these p^rsents)
As well for & on the behalfe of
themselves as for & on ye behalfe of
their Respective Indyans or People for whom they are
      Concerned

Have granted Bargained Sold & Delivered
And by these p^rsents doe fully
Clearly
& absolutely
grant bargain Sell & Deliv^r unto the said
William Penn
his Heirs & Assignes
forever

All That or those Tract or Tracts of Land
lyeing & being
in the Province of Pennsylvania aforesaid
Beginning at a certain white Oake
in the Land now in the Tenure of John Wood
& by him called ye Gray Stones
over against the ffals of Dellaware River
And Soe from thence

up by the River Side
to a Corner marked Spruce Tree with the Letter P
at the ffoot of a mountaine
And from the said Corner marked Spruce Tree
along by the Ledge or ffoot of the Mountaines
West-North-West
to a Corner white oake marked
With the Letter P standing
by the Indyan Path that Leads

to an Indyan Towne
called Play Wicky & near the head
of a Creek called Tosissink
And from thence

westward to the Creek called Neshammonyes Creek
And along by the said Neshammonyes Creek
unto the River Dellaware
alies Makerick Kitton
And soe bounded
by the Said Maine River
to the Said first menconed white Oake in John Woods
    Land,

And all those Islands called or knowne
by the severall names of Matimicunck Island
Sapssincke Island,
& Orecktons Island lyeing
or being in the Said River Dellaware,

Together alsoe with all & Singuler Isles
Islands Rivers
Riveletts Creeks
waters Ponds
Lakes Plaines Hills
Mountaynes Meadowes
purtennces whasover to the Said Tract of Land
Marrishes Swamps
Trees
Woods
Mynes
Mineralls & Appurtennces whatsoever to the Said Tract or
    Tracts of Land
belonging or in anywise Apperteyning And

ye Reverson & Reversons Remaind^r & Remaind^{r}s thereof
And all ye Estate

Right   Tytle   Interest
use   pperty Clayme
& Demand whatsoever as well of them the Said Indyan
    Sachamakers
(ptyes to these p^rsents) as of all & every other
the Indyans Concerned therein
or in any pte pcell thereof

TO HAVE & TO HOLD
the said Tract & Tracts of Land
Island & all & every other the said Granted p^rmisses
with their & every of their Appurtennces
unto ye sayd
William Penn His Heires & Assignes forever
To the onely ppr use & behoofe of
ye sayd William Penn his Heires & Assignes
forevermore

And the sayd Indyan Sachamakers
& their Heires & Successo^rs
& every one of them the Said Tract
or Tracts of Land Islands & all
& every the Said granted p^rmisses
with their & every of their Appurtennces
unto the Said William Penn
his Heires & Assign^es forever

against them
the Sayd Indyan Sachamakers
thir Heires & Successo^rs clayming
or to claime
any Right   Tytle   or Estate
into or out of ye said Granted p^rmisses
or any pte prcell thereof
shall & will warrant
& forever defend
by these p^rsents

IN WITNESSE whereof
the said ptys to these p^rsent Indentures
Interchangeably
have sett their hands & Seales
the day & yeare ffirst above written
1682

The m^rke of

Idquayhom

The m^rke of

Janottowe

The m^rke of

Idquaquon

The m^rke of

Sahoppe

The m^rke of

Merkekowen

The m^rke of
Oreck ton for
himself &
Nannacussey

The m^rke
of

Shaurwaughon

The m^rke of

Swanpisse

The m^rke of

Nahoosey

The m^rke
of

Tomackhickon

The m^rke of

Westkekitt

The marke of

Kowyorkhikon

25

Before there was a Philadelphia
There was a Philadelphia lawyer.

He had read the law at Lincoln's Inn,
Had managed his father's estates in County Cork.

He knew about warranty deeds and quitclaim deeds,
Chancery suits and litigations.

Knew what to read between the lines.
Did the Indians know how to read?

Did they know they'd forfeited forever
Their rites on the grave-mounds of their ancestors?

Did they know they'd given up the grounds
To their hunting-grounds and happy-hunting-grounds?

They didn't even get to keep
Picnic rights to their own property.

Property? What is the Earth
That they can sell or trade in her,

Their Mother who has given them birth,
Whose hair of leaves bears fruit and berries

Which the first mothers gathered.
No one among the living owns her body,

She is vast, abundant, self-renewing.
The living hold this Earth the fathers held

In trust for them, for their children, and for theirs.
They share her with these peaceful Friends who bring

A strange tongue and great possessions. They are few
And for a day. The Earth shall last forever.

26

'When the Purchase was agreed, great Promises
past between us of Kindness and good Neighborhood,
and that the Indians and English
must live in Love,
as long as the Sun gave light.

'Which done, another made a Speech to the Indians,
in the Name of all the *Sachamakers* or Kings,
first to tell them what was done;
next, to charge and command them, To Love the
        Christians,
and particularly live in Peace with me, and the People
        under my Government:
At every sentence of which they shouted, and said,
Amen, in their way.'

27

They would call on him at Pennsbury,
His Manor House beside the River,

With feathers at their ears and quivered flints,
Loin clouts hanging from their waists on thongs,

With ceremonious step of moccasin
Upon the graveled walks between shrub roses

Past topiary trees. At the end of the Garden
Miquon (as they called their friend) arises

To greet them: He, still lean and strong, the courtier,
And they like Romans, now salute each other.

His servants hasten to attend them: Tables
Of buckwheat cakes on platters, sides of venison

Are prepared and trundled out. Meantime
The Proprietor and his guests in contests vie,

He leaping on the lawn as they leap:
They leap far from a standing start

But he, Miquon, their good friend and host,
He leaps farther, to their cheers.

II

AN OPENING
OF JOY

I am Alpha and Omega, the first and the last:
and what thou seest, write in a book
and send it . . . unto Philadelphia . . .

28

We must crane our necks to raise
Our eyes to his gaze.

Calder's statue towers on City Hall,
His pedestal.

He looms immense, remote. How could he
Dream into being this wrangling 'City

Of Brotherly Love,' this flawed
Commonweal—was it

Through excess of zeal
Or the soulstorm of an age

Our own cannot conceive?
Who hasn't heard the tale—but Time

Wears out our words, our ways of saying
Age as men do, grow incontinent

And die; and History,
That always wants another telling,

Puts before us
The players, a choice of motives and their acts,

What was given, what received,
The facts or the presumed facts,

But omits the Chorus
Whose clear song extracts

From the furor of their passions
The truth of what is real.

Now I
Whom this tale charges

To gather clues, make out
Its ghostly trail

In forests long hewn down,
Buried deep beneath

A mulch of leaves
Once crisp as paper, nurturing

The hoarded purpose nothing
But the pattern that they hold

While hiding it can show—
Whatever it is,

It is this particular design
That grows from these

Intractable pieces of deed
And real imaginings,

Only in part resembling
Other imaginings or deeds. These change

A past shared with others
Into an original

Sense of life to come:
Whatever this

Heap of pieces made
Of language is,

It takes the shape
Of its necessities,

Not to be known by others'
Form or name.

In this legend what precedes
The Founder's fame?

—Recital of his father's deeds, the body
Of fact before the spirit's dream.

29

At last the full sail of my verse can swell
With martial airs, and I of triumph tell:
Bomb and firepot, volley and blazing deck
As the *Royal Charles* sails past the wallowing wreck
Of insolent Opdam's best ship of the line.

Wherefore these tardy strophes, now, of mine,
When poets of that court were prompt to praise
Both Duke and Victory within nine days?
Fierce, godly, young! Mars he resembled, when
Jove sends him down to scourge perfidious men!
What wonder may not English valour work,
Led by the example of victorious York?
Yet, fealty owing neither King nor Duke,
I no preferment seek, nor fear rebuke,
But would recount, in verse, once more, the oft-
Hailed sea-fight won by James at Lowestoft.

Consider: Though he was Lord High Admiral, James
Had scarcely sailed a dinghy on the Thames,
Yet led to sea a hundred and a score
Of ships well-armed. So Dukes may play at war,
And crowd the *Royal Charles* with gentlemen.
Of all his captains, only four and ten
Had tasted enemy shot mixed with their brine.
Who, then, is charged with holding to the line
This great Armada? Whose the stratagem

That guides these quondam sea-dogs, and brings them
Home to Greenfleet and the crowds' acclaim?
There's one aboard, the Dutch, hearing whose name,
Would quail; who seized Jamaica from the pomp
Of Spain, and boldly trounced renowned Van Tromp.

Was this the reason, when his scapegrace son
From Greenfleet to Whitechapel late had run
As courier, bearing tidings to the Crown,
That Charles skips out of bed in but his gown
And royal slippers, saying, 'Oh! It's you?
How is Sir William?' Was that just his due
Since he was owed both salary and outlay
For fitting ships for which the Crown can't pay?
Or, that in Cromwell's time, he gave the king
Clandestine loyalty, helping to bring
His monarch home from France, and was made knight
On shipboard? Now, he'll oversee the fight
While at his side the noble Duke wins fame.

Who else sails on the *Royal Charles?* I'll name
Companionable scourges of the sea:
The Earls of Falmouth and of Muskerry
And Burlington's son, Mr. Boyle; another
Is Harry Brouncker, who's a Viscount's brother
And Gentleman-in-Waiting to the Duke;
What here avails them ruff, stick, or peruke
When from the crow's nest comes the lookout's cry,
'*Sail to windward!*'? Soon the line where sky
And sea are met is studded with the sails
Of Holland's men-of-war, on freshening gales
Approaching in precise formation fast.
Captains Cox and Harman now make haste
To raise the tacking flags, at Penn's command,
And now the English turn downwind to stand
Against the foe's first furious cannonade,

But darkness falls, the issue is delayed
Till sunrise. Foretelling where the Dutch would lurk,
Penn crowds and closes! This is fearful work,
Breaking the enemy's mighty line. Ashore,
Though London hears the intermittent roar
Of cannon on the sea-wind, none can tell
Whose ship, ablaze, stains Channel skies, until
A sloop brings news—A glorious victory!

Not yet does London learn the toll at sea—
Right on the deck the Duke is splashed with gore
As a whirring chain-shot through the rigging tore
And cut down Falmouth, Muskerry, and Boyle:
A bloody taste of battle for the royal
Command. But cheer—a British shot, by keen
Good aim, or luck, blows up the magazine
Of Admiral Opdam's flagship, and the Dutch
Heel for the Texel, English taking such
As lag behind the protection of the night.
Thus by the Duke the Dutch are put to flight.

But now, while London's bells clang Victory,
The second dawn finds England still at sea,
The Dutchmen's shallower craft safe in their haven.
On History's scroll this triumph shan't be graven,
For since Phoenicia, none can claim defeat
Without destruction of the rival's fleet.
And when the second courier sloop has landed
How can the first dispatch be countermanded?
More modest claims would make the Duke a fool;
Better prevent the barbs of ridicule
From puncturing his false triumph's balloon.
But all the world will wonder, late or soon,
How came the British fleet to shorten sail
In darkness (the next thing to turning tail)
As though their Lord High Admiral's taste of fire

Had stifled, in that royal breast, desire
For further danger—Sir William having said
The Dutch fight always harder, being bled.

Let Pepys, Penn's rival and the Navy's Clerk,
Tell how the Parliament probed through the murk
Of this strange circumstance, after two years'
Expense of honour, money, blood, and tears:
'Who gave that order? The Duke had gone below;
Sir William, certain of their course, did so
As well, being weary, and troubled by the gout.
Captain Cox, next in command, did doubt
Brouncker's entreaty that he countervail
The Duke, for whose sake he should shorten sail.
Next after Cox is Harman, to whom Harry
Says, 'twould please the King, were he to tarry
(Brouncker mindful, too, of the great distress
Felt by the Duchess, and the Duke's mistress);
Rash accident may slay the Duke, unless
You hold back, out of range, and do not press—
At last prevailed on, Harman shortens sail.
The men of Parliament vow not to fail
To send unto the Tower—methinks the block—
Harry, or Harman, soon as his ship shall dock
And they examine him. Brouncker's confessed
He so advised, believing that course best,
Did so, not in the Duke's, but his own name
—Thus Harman's compliance is the greater blame
If that's the way the wind blows. Of these men
Him I most wonder at's Sir W. Pen,
Who on the morrow noticed not, he said,
His orders disobeyed. And so to bed.'

The Duke's own testimony claims he, neither,
Knew they'd lost such way in such good weather,
And Harman, he avows, declined the demand

Of Brouncker, save it be by Penn's command,
Whereon below awhile the courtier went;
Returning, claims that he this time was sent
By the Duke of York to order him, stand by.
Not thinking that a gentleman would lie,
Good Captain Harman did as he was told.
One timorous courtier thus undid the bold
Seamanship of Penn, and cast his master
Adrift in a political near-disaster.
Yet, in the end, when all's been heard and said,
No one's sent to the Tower, or lost his head;
What I most wonder at is how such men
As the Admiral Duke and Fleet Commander Penn
Could not know that their ship a sluggard sailed,
Nor by whose wish a great campaign had failed;
What's also hard to fathom is, not one
Of those aboard unspliced what had been done;
Though currents of ill rumor raged and swirled,
They trimmed their sails, the truth in silence furled,
Silence their armor against all dispute,
Guarding the Navy's and the Duke's repute.

But wonder not Sir William was discreet
That moment forward, his loyalty to the Fleet,
To his Lord High Admiral and Stuart King
Unswerving, more in this than anything
—As they well knew. To James, patron and friend,
With dying breath Sir William would commend
His son and namesake, whom he yet still loved
Though for his stubborn folly still reproved:
The boy's conceit, plebeian godliness—
That headstrong faith a father's great distress,
Yet on his deathbed gave him certain measure
Of satisfaction, if not full-hearted pleasure;
Young William, being imprisoned in the Tower
For challenging the arbitrary power
Of magistrates, as he stood in the dock

Well proved himself a chip off the Old Block:
With his father's courage defends his Quaker cause
And challenges the courts to keep the laws!
Sir William paid, the week before he died,
The fine that freed his son, in hopes his pride
Might see the light and that good sense would bring
Him, hat in hand, before his Duke and King.

30

Whose is the kingdom, what the glory?
It is not easy, being son

To the hero of the English nation.
One thing is sure: You'll never go to sea.

Your father is master of this world
Where men twist their blades for power;

His admiral's flag commands how many bloodied tides
Where the dead sway in the streaked water.

Christ has banished Mars. Yet you are torn
Between your father and the Son.

Your soul delights in clarity,
In oneness.

The cost of the care of the soul is this,
You must withdraw rejoicing from the wind
Arriving to caress you from a place
Horizons hide, tousling the meadows, leaving
Unannounced for some still sierra
Where it may bring rains; you must forsake
The clearing after, and the glisten on
Each leaf and stem, the yarrow nodding in its
Dewy mantle, the blossoms in a woven
Elegance of white with lacy leaves
Still intricately clutching beads of rain;
Withdraw your pleasure from the clouds convening
On the ridges of the hill, nor mind

Their annunciation of the tournament
Of colors of the evening when the caucus
Of white-throat's whistles, blackbird's juicy chirrs
And the choughs' rude scoffs are hushed, all hushed
But for the far-off pealing of reclusive
Nightingale—to none of which you listen,
Giving your awareness only
To the soul;

Life springs so abundantly in you,
In the thick foliage of your own vigor you are lost

In confusion: whether
To let your beloved father espalier

Your spirit in those shapes that should adorn
The mannered gardens of a loose-lived King

Or to lop off and prune, yourself, all that excrescent wildness
So that your soul,

Reaching in purer air than father breathes,
So high above the earth its branches

Splashed by the sun's brimming ewer of light
Will, when that goes out, shine on with light

More pure, more bright than nature's source
Or any seen by natural sight—

Still, would you not enjoy and flourish
Under the preferments father schemes to grant you?

But your soul spurns the dusty bones of the world's dead hours,
It's the cool waters of eternity you long for.

The plaints, and worse, the urges of your body
You must put down.
You must not think of women and their bodies,
The breasts that bulge above their bodices,
The mysterious aggravation that their voices
Rallying and falling like birdsong in summer rain
Bestir in your tumultuous heart. You must
Not think
Of how beneath the giddying ringlets of her hair,
Head cocked, eyes laughing, she is poised
To wreak
Invisible stabs, a burning in the blood and breath
Caught as in a noose the heart is caught
For the cost
Of the care of the soul is this:

O if you could but banish your own body, leaving
Only your spirit to inhale

Pure light.
Your sorrowful

Cries afflict the Lord,
Your knees have worn grooves in the floorboards.

Within yourself the bolt slides
On the dark gaol

Where the woman you would touch betrays
Your soul, your soul.

How endure
Knowledge of your own desire?

Purity, cries the voice within, *Purity!*
But the Church is of this world, corrupt with its corruptness.

Charity, Charity, pleads your inward tongue
But the Puritans to all not Puritans wield

The hard stave of their unforgiveness.
'Seeing as yet no such thing,' your pen scrawls,

'As the primitive spirit, the true church on earth,
And being ready to faint concerning

My hope
For the restitution of all things,

After this the Glory
Of the World overtook me,

I was even ready
To give myself up to it—'

31

INSTRUCTIONS TO A PAINTER
OF PORTRAITS IN DUBLIN, 1666

Not the Seeker or the Swain
The likeness that your Art should feign,
    Nor Scholar's abstract gaze
    Who gropes in learning's maze;

But paint the purposed brow of one
Who sternest Duty did not shun,
    Whose twenty-second year
    Was proof against all fear,

As, worthy of his Father's fame,
At Carrickfergus made a name
    With the Vice-Regal Court,
    Storming the rebels' fort.

Though he would grasp Ormonde's reward
And lead the Kinsale troop of guard,
    His Father, worldlier far,
    Forbids he hide his star.

No great career will soon be made
In that provincial palisade;
    His light let shine among
    The well-born and the strong.

Who knows how high his son may rise
In the Duke's favor, the King's eyes?
    Show, then, the eager lip
    That's savored its first sip

From glory's goblet; at the throat
Let fall a flowing, fringed jabot
    To soften the severe
    Cast of cavalier

In iron corselet, but suppress
The look of inward pensiveness
    That clouds his unlined face
    And would all pride displace.

Your subject will attend the throne
And make this treacherous world his own,
    Mastering those arts
    That fit a man of parts:

32

33

From posing in Dublin, pleased with his own likeness he
    returns to the accounts, the rents, the litigious papers—
It's on his father's business he comes to Cork,
and a button's missing on his sleeve as when he came here
    once with mother
and there's the shop where she had taken him,
shop of a Quaker woman, buttons, bolts of cloth, shirts,
    coats, stockings, pins,
—Strange she finds it, strange indeed, that he so familiarly
    should speak
—this fancy gentleman she'd never seen—of what she'd sold
    and said
ten years before, until 'You surely do recall
my father, Sir William Penn of Castle Macroom?' and then
she laughs aloud to think of the shy, hangback lad peeping
    behind
his jovial mother, him now grown up so manly, handsome,
so much a man of the world, she says,

while sewing on his button. Is it remembering, or
    something in himself today
recalls the Publisher of Truth his father asked to preach
once, at Macroom—he'd judge, himself, what roused the
    countryside
to such a passion—this sectary who held the Seed of Light
is in us by God's Will, no priests being needed by the soul
to interpose their altar, surplice, wafer, chants, or prayers
between a Christian and his God.
'It's many a mile I'd walk to hear again
the tongue of Thomas Loe,' says Penn, 'who made

my father's servant, Black Anthony from Jamaica, weep,
and my father wept, and I too,
on hearing him, shed tears.'

'Thee need not go so far if thee will stop
this night in Cork, for here Friend Thomas
waits upon the Lord tomorrow.' His father's business
        stretches
with tedium the interminable hours, a strange
expectancy within him whirring
like a single swallow in an empty barn.
Sleepless night in Crown & Garter,
belfry throbbing with his apprehension
of the coming of a Word . . . the sky
pales, then blushes. Cart creaks on cobbles
echo from drowsy walls. He must
stride out past shops and houses, beyond
the cottages, the farms, to walk awhile
alone,
no one, no thing,
no thought

between him and the brightening clouds.
So on this hill of furze and heather, grey rock
and scattered flock of browsing sheep
in the vastness of the dewy air the mist swirls,
the sweetly mocking bell-song of the hours' chimes brought
brokenly by winds across the heath from
distant spires. Time,
time of this world. Disconsolate longing
floods him near to tears. He
turns, trudges to house of Friends.
Low-ceilinged room.
In bright-buckled shoes and velvet breeches,
shining scabbard and wide hat with plumes
he sits, a gamecock among silent chats and wrens,
and looks about for Thomas Loe. No pulpit,

all sit side by side. There, on the bench
among the rest, in silence.
Stillness spreads until it all but bursts with promise while
the humming world is still,
still, and they are famished
for a word
which they unspeakingly await—

34

Silence, more
eloquent than
speech: the un-
spoken word
wiser than our

earnest trials
to say, to find
in the mind's hoard
praise that reveals
perfections known

and not diminished
in the telling—
in the silences
between speech and halt
speech, beseech

a gift of tongues
that words bear
witness, true
to what we hear
chiefly in silence

before and after
speech now, as
these letters
whiten the space
surrounding them.

35

'Open Thou my lips,' the Prophet said, 'and then
My mouth shall praise the Lord.' But not till then.

The Preparation of the Heart is of the Lord.
The Answer of the Tongue is of the Lord.

Since God is Spirit, the Divine in us
Uses a dialect whose dictates we hear

As He heeds us, Who needs no speech to hear.
What forms of ours are adequate to God?

There is a faith the world overcomes,
And there is faith that overcomes the world.

—That is the text!—the rest, elaboration.
No one set down the tropes of Thomas Loe,

No other word of his that spelled His Word
On which Penn's life henceforth is commentary.

A coal from God's Altar must kindle us,
No sacrifice acceptable without True Fire.

36

None of the masters would lend themselves or their vessels
to such a work as this;
but in Captain Fudge, a man who was known to say
that for a fee he'd transport his own mother to Hell,
the Sheriffs found a mariner
fit for their business.

> More than five men meeting
> To wait upon the Lord
> Without the Church of England
> Have unsheathed treason's sword,
> More than five men meeting,

So fifty-five were hauled then out of Newgate,
thrust in a barge at Blackfriars and sent downstream
to Bugby's Hole, where lay his ship
the *Black-Spread-Eagle*.
When the barge approached (the Captain ashore,
dead drunk in his stewe) the crew refused
to force any Person aboard; and the Prisoners
declined to take an active part
in their own Transportation.
The officers then used high words
to the crew, saying, *These Prisoners
are the King's Goods*, but the Mariners neither
would move nor be moved to abuse them.
The Turnkeys got only four aboard that day
and were obliged to return the rest to Newgate.

On the 4th of the Moon called August
a second time they were pressed into the Barge.

The sailors once more refusing, from the Tower
were Soldiery sent to haul them aboard
and they were punched, dragged, kicked, some
like malt-sacks heaved by the arms and legs
till into the ship they tumbled, all
thirty-seven of the Men and the eighteen Women,

> Hale them into court.
> Not one will doff his hat?
> Such scorn of Magistrate
> Will undermine the State.
> Hale them into court

condemned to seven years' Transportation
to the Island of Jamaica. When,
at their Trial, one, William Brand, inquired,
'Was it a Crime deserving Banishment
to meet to serve the Lord?'

> Like Jesuits they plead.
> To the King will they not swear
> Allegiance? They're in league
> With Traitors everywhere.
> Like Jesuits they plead,

And the Judge gave answer, *Yes,*
yes, for the Law,
the Law is against it.

> How fares the English Church,
> How well thrives England's throne
> Until the law crush
> Blasphemy, sedition,
> All such misprision?

So all the men were crammed
together between the decks where none could stand;

close was the air, and foul
with heat, with body reek, the stench
hung like a fog around her anchorage,
and her Captain was seized and imprisoned for debt.
Then Pestilence spread on board the Ship
and for seven months the scummy water
slapped her planks as she lolled at her mooring.
At last the *Black-Spread-Eagle* made for the Mouth of the
    Thames
And by then of her cargo
were twenty-seven in the shallow marshes
buried below Gravesend.

With a new Captain the Vessel cleared the Downs,
touched at Plymouth, then for the Indies sailed—
Five hours at sea, a Privateer
boards and claims the *Black-Spread-Eagle,* half
of her prisoners and her crew put over,
and the Dutch pirates sail the rest as their prize ship north,
north to Bergen Harbor. There
three weeks ice-bound she lies at the quay.
Word goes forth in the strange Norwegian tongue
that there are Friends aboard her,
and so come many curious near to hear their doctrines.
And so the Seed of Light is sown
and interpreted amongst another people.

At last the *Eagle* sails to Horn,
the Dutch intending that for them
the English would exchange their Prisoners.
But seeing their countrymen refuse them ransom
nor wanting them brought back to Holland
if captured by another Privateer,
they give these Quakers each Passports,
Certificates of Safety,
and send them home.

That year
the London streets were black with buzzards,
black with flies.
The death-cart slow, and slow the tolling bell,
heavy the judgment on a generation
wicked, and profane.
These banished few, arriving, join their brethren
to offer thanks for safe deliverance
in His mercy, in the public room
beside the Tavern called the Bull and Mouth.
For two hours the People were together and peaceably kept
    their Meeting,
ready to dismiss, when in came roaring
Major-General Brown with a Party of Men, Pikes and Swords
    drawn
and when they were entered among the People they cried
Shut the Door, make it fast!
the Officer having in hand a Club a Yard long,
for size and weight as much as he could handle,
he and his Party then fell to strike and wound the People
    fearfully
in the most unmerciful manner ever beheld in this City
in Time of Peace, and neither Man nor Woman
Young nor Old they spared but into the Streets
they haled them, cut and bruised
and beat some down to the ground where lay
six or eight half-dead by sore blows. They knocked
one down five times, and such was the cry
of the Lookers-on (for amongst them were abundance in the
    Street
that were no Quakers), many got grievous wounds
for their pitiful words,
who cried out, *Shame, shame, that ever these Things*
should be seen in London,
for the Blood lay visible in the Streets
and running down their Faces and Shoulders

and one, John Trowell, by Reason of Bruises and Blows
which inwardly settled upon him
for the Man that beat him, kicked and trampled
violently upon his Heart, is dead.
When it was asked of the Soldiers, *Why they would be so cruel
to their Neighbors,* one
replied, Nay, we are more merciful than we ought,
for we have orders to kill.

The day after these beatings, Solomon Eccles
made of himself at Bartholomew Fair
a sign: stark naked
he walked, upon his head
a pan ablaze with brimstone, crying,
Repent! Remember Sodom!
And on the First-Day following, the Quakers
in peace again assembled at the Bull and Mouth to meet.
As soldiers barred the door, they held their worship
in the common street,

> More than five men meeting
> To wait upon the Lord
> Without the Laws of England,
> Have unsheathed Treason's sword,
> More than five men meeting.

37

He lies in the nave of darkness where the night
Holds its black breath and the blood pounds
Behind his eyes in streaks of red heat lightning

And his body makes known the individual fatigues
Of the foot, of the back, of the shoulder, the brain
Which interrupted sleep has not assuaged

And without thinking, thoughts as effortless
As breath press on him while his mouth fills
With exhalations from the mouth of the darkness

—Down a littered street all doors are barred,
Crosses chalked on walls, and nothing moves
But ragbone horse straining at laden hearse

While ravens perch on rooftree and the evening
Cringes, pierced by mortal moans, the shrieks
Of the new widow, the dying and the doomed:

It is himself he sees watching the scene
Yet he is in it, is carried from the house
And thrown by hooded bearers on the waggon,

And now the death-cart turns at palace gate,
It is an open carriage in the courtyard
With him in armor in it, and his sword,

Descending, plumes sweeping the ground, he bows,
Obedient servant, low before Milord
By rote, though rotes of pomp and man's debasement

Weigh on his heart with grief, with Sabbath grief
For the lost simplicity of true behaving
Where all's dissembling—at the window, glare

Of flames that creep up gables, race down thatch
Then comb the roofs and leap the narrow streets
As flaking showers of sparks pelt down on wharves,

Ships, bales, taverns, shops all crackling
And where were houses, stand black skeletons;
Within, flames dance their avenging dance

As the blistering sky roars with the world's death-pain.
Then glare dissolves and he lies in the dark
In the moment without movement, the awaiting

Acceptance of the unavoidable:
Out of that cold shuddering blackness where
The aching mind is blind and feelings freeze,

Where only the terror of confusion is possible,
Confusion and the terror of the nothingness
The world is that knows no love—

With a rush beyond the mind's grasp
(The world is death and ashes without love)
He feels his body quake as though a Hand

Grasps his neckbone,
                    holds him
            to the Light:

38

As William Penn am I
In this life till I die.
In this life, what is real,
The body, or the soul?
My father whom I love
Is not my Father above;
His soldier's, courtier's strife
Not my life, or the Life:
This flesh which he begot,
These senses that I feel,
These appetites, are not
The Holy Seed in me,
But as a wooden bowl
Holds water pure and fresh
Dropped from crystal cloud,
Its clarity the same
As when from Heaven it came,
Until I wear a shroud
This vessel of my flesh
Is the chalice of my soul.

39

Takes on the habit now
of this Society, among them finds
true fellowship and love unfeigning.
Avoids all signs of worldly rank,
all men his equals in God's sight.
Refuses, as Christ bids, to swear.
For a Christian's YEA is YEA, his NAY is NAY,
And for not swearing oaths are the Friends cast into prison.

Of this peculiar people's testimony
another is, not fighting
but suffering, since they affirm
all wars and fightings come of the lusts
of men's own hearts, not
the spirit of Christ Jesus.
And for this the King and his minions
who wage wars to enlarge his dominions
cast the Friends into prison.

His testimony to peace gives Penn concern.
What is George Fox's counsel?
He'd be as true as any, but wears his sword
and this, among the Friends, seems vain,
a provocation. Yet the sword
has saved his life: when on a street in Paris
a drunken gentleman for some supposed slight
drew on him, with that blade
Penn, good swordsman, disarmed the man
and spared his life
who would have taken his for nothing.

Now Fox looks sideways at this Gentleman Commoner
so lately to his doctrines won,
still in buckled shoes, a courtier's hat,
a sword,
and says,

'I advise thee to wear it as long as thou canst.'

'Where is thy sword, Friend William?' Fox inquires
on their meeting soon again. 'Oh,' says Penn,
'I have taken thy advice,'
                          —armed henceforth
in the manner of the Friends
against the powers and dominions of this world:

40

Clang. Scuffle, scuffle, scuffle. Steps
diminish down the winding stair, then no
sound in the damp, stale air save distant
lurch and clatter of carts on cobbles, muffled
cries—boatmen down on the river, or
hawkers calling 'Sweet cakes!' beneath the eaves.
Then silence. Only the beat, the beat, the beat
of his own pulse breaks on his temples as he peers
through narrow grate. A blue-green fly hums
past the windowslit, its back and belly
dazzling as a molten bead, a-buzz
on invisible wings, exulting in its free
swoops toward earth, then into the blazing sun
and back, in intricate figures in the air until
of a sudden, on a whim, it darts
through stone-and-iron slits and comes to rest
on the lip of the waterjug within his cell.
He could snatch it, quick, hold this creature
prisoner in his cupped hand, his fingers barring
all such fancy flights—but would the fly
still rejoice with imaginary loops
and pirouettes in the crystal air, just as
he, confined, yet celebrates his soul's
freedom, with which no man can tamper? At his
first movement, the fly leaps and
is gone.
   Leaving him with silence, alone
in the dank cell. Heavy, each breath is heavy.
His spirit is borne down. How can his sufferings
be worthy in this ducal cell, so little
like the wretched rat's-hole gaol in Launceston
where villagers threw offal on George Fox,

86

or the cell where young Parnell, true to his Faith,
was beaten, starved, and died. Surely the Lord
calls each to serve from his own circumstance
to do His will. Initiate of Oxford,
cradle of casuistries, his thought
made subtler by savant Amyraut's *sagesse*,
as courtier and advocate he serves those dear
and humble Friends whose sufferings are far
more worthy than his. The Lord commands
we love our enemies, yet he enjoys
wrangling against the wrongs of the realm to bare
the malice of bishops and magistrates. His learning
pricks their libels, for Christ's sword
is spiritual, like His Kingdom.
                                    Why, then,
hard upon his heart does a hand press down,
iron-gloved with gloom, a grip, as of guilt?
Was it futile to fly against father's affection
till father barred him from home? Fear
of unfaithfulness to father and Friends
assails him. His heart
is a muffled drum.

                A vacant space
                a bare oak
                dead leaves rattling
                in cold wind
                each shadow
                casting
                a deeper shadow

                on the chilled
                shroud
                of his own skin
                and his proud will
                sheathed
                in black ice

—Where is his soul in this dark place?

The silence
and the emptiness
around him
are within him.
He is a piece of the nothingness.

If he could only pray—

Is it morning?

A contentment he cannot explain swells in him.

The sky suddenly softens, all airy and fresh and of infinite
  blue.

Alight with the burble of birds are the brambles, the bushes,

As above him a great tree lifts its trunk and broad arms,

Its huge head of green swaying against Heaven's
  garden-gate

And he feels the Lord open his soul with a love that
  embraces all

Beasts of the field and the forest—his heart

Reaches beyond the horizon's rim.

By a river he sees, in white raiments arrayed, a great people
  gathered,

And their faces are toward him—

Who are all these assembled, and what are they
  seeking?

He sees himself on the mountain, yet stands in their midst

Sensing the soul in each separate person among them.

And many a manner of man is among them,

Flourishing in amity, and Friends with the rest.

All get on together with good cheer and gossip

As at a fair or market-day men meet and speak frankly.

These folk with their myriad desires and husbanded skills,

Some open-hearted, some feckless, some shrewd with their
farthings and pence,

Quarrelsome among themselves, yet affectionate as well, and
capable of the greatest goodness,

What do they want in this life and why has history
condemned them

To suffer such woe in the world who might better live
lovingly?

See, the people of the world, their motley sects, garbs,
occupations,

The men of England and the women, and those of all other
lands and tongues,

And these bronzed folk who know not of Christ and dwell
in bark huts in the woods,

Those who bring with them their Bibles, money-ledgers,
trivets and pots, their harrows, their ploughs,

And those who pluck from the forest their fruit as did Eve
and Adam of old—

His eyes see through their garments of cloth and their
fleshly garments,

His soul is aware of the soul in each of their bodies,

The thirst of his soul that seeks refreshment and longs to be
made whole

By a draught from the pure well that waters the Seed of
    Light

Is the thirst of their spirits, and the Light and the dew
    refresh him

With the knowing that he, and they, severally and each, are
    all souls

Seeking to grow in goodness and merit salvation

In brotherly love,

We who are made in God's image and are therefore
    brothers.

It is to himself that the Chieftain directly is speaking

And the bursting sun sends down its breakers of light as
    before,

The great tree thrusts its green withes toward Heaven,

The twittering in the bushes trills, is hushed, then small
    birdshapes dart off

And he knows that although he has never heard such a
    dialect before

He knows what the Indian King is saying, and what in
    return he will say;

He is both hearing this language of sounds like the plashing
    of narrow-hoofed deer in a stream,

Preparing with care and diplomacy his own phrases in that
    very tongue,

And aware of himself there and of himself here, watching,

And not yet has he wondered what is the name of this
    place

90

And why is he there and of what is he witness and of what
the participant

And why his heart brims to the breaking with the sureness
and nearness of a love

He will always remember

As in a well-pool the color of Heaven is clearer than
Heaven's own hue

Until, at a dropped stone, the image is broken.

Everything will be sorted out in good time.

All of his perplexities and self-doubts will dissolve.

And in peace they shall live together.

And if all of history does not prove this to be so

It is time to begin

To prove it is so.

Time is dissolved and he knows that the he who is
watching himself is a witness

To the destiny that will await him

In which he will move

Out of the sufferings of the world that is fallen.

He is alight with his knowledge in which all propositions
are fused in one arc of brightness

As all colors are fused in one arc of brightness unbroken

Save when a prism of droplets from Heaven spreads it apart

And each of its colors is pure and imperturbable,

The truth of its violet as true as the truth of its faintest
   blue,

And all in the pulse of pure light alive and shining.

In the Lord's love for each person

Is His revelation

Perpetual and unending,

And they shall come together in a city,

> City of lovely purposes
> upholding balconies
> espaliered on walls
> and windows
> reeling with cerulean light—
>
> where each breath's an anthem and each glance a
>   hymn,
> here is the spirit's home.
>
> Folks crowd round him
> as many as the green and gilded leaves
> of the tall oak
> that glimmer in the sun and sway
> lofted by the importunate summer wind
>
> down boulevards receding
> toward the domes
> that thrust their curves and tips against the sky.
>
> This light
> indwelling in the soul
> and bursting forth
>
> —Is this the color of joy?—

For the Lord is the home of the soul

And the world which is far from God

Is history, the body's prison,

But the House of Stuart shall deed to the House of Penn

A Province

Of the New World

Where history has not yet begun,

A city of brotherly love.

Then as though he outleapt his own strength across crags in
a dazzle of air,

With a surging billow within his being

His mortal frame is ashake and atremble at the touch of the
Hand of the Lord

And he knows he is blessed by the bounty of Love without
end

And his soul is merged with the ceaseless splendor of
unending light.

III

THE STRUCTURE
OF REALITY

Who cares what the fact was,
when we have made a constellation of it
to hang in heaven an immortal sign?

—EMERSON, 'HISTORY'

41

This opening of joy
—the motion of the Lord
upon the soul—

makes possible
in our life in time
an intimation of that Light

which that of God causes to glow
in every soul.
Henceforth we cherish

the legend that is to come,
the vision that precedes
us as we go

through the wicket of the possible.
It is time to begin
to prove it is so.

Him that overcometh will I make
a pillar in the temple, I will write
upon him the name

of the city . . . There is the blaze
of history's trail,
where the tree is slashed

in the dark wood, tentatively
marking the faded track
of those who came here long ago

intending good,
tending to what necessity
seemed to make the one

choice possible
whenever there was choice.
Listen—

in the clamor of their voices,
in the muddle of their deeds,
see, there's a design

where words like fallen leaves,
like falls of snow have muffled,
have baffled and half-hidden

the structure of reality:

42

Good King Charley swigged his hops and his barley
  And a jolly old king was he,

  'by the Grace of God, Defender of the Faith, &c.'

He called for his Chancellor and Ministers of State
  And he called for his Mistresses three.

Now the King of Hearts plays at Whists and Darts
  And holds Banquets and Balls at his Court
For his Gentlemen of Parts and his High-Breasted Tarts,
  And be damned if the money runs short,

And be damned if the Tailor or the Victualler Royal
  Or the Cavalry, or men in the Fleet
Make a tasteless turmoil because it's been such a while
  Ere they had wherewithal to eat.

See, here, straight as a staff comes the Lord's mooncalf,
  The son of dear Admiral Penn!
With his hat on his poll he is bound to be droll
  Though the Crown rules more tractable men—

    When Penn attended him the King removed his
      crown.
    Asked why he did so, H.M. replied, 'Friend Penn,
    I bare my head because it is the custom here,
    when in the presence of the King,
    that only *one* of us be covered.'
                                      —Much merriment

at this sally from the king whose wit
amused the wits *The Soldier's Pleasure*
and *The Country Wife* amused . . .

Now with all due respect, against the Conventicle Act
    Or is't for Quakers in gaol that he pleads?
Welladay, now it sounds like those Sixteen Thousand Pounds
    The Throne owes his Da' that he needs—

But see, William Quaker won't shipwreck the Exchequer
    Or sink King and Chancellor yet:
He requests and receives a quitclaim

        'Whereas our Trustie and well beloved Subject,
        William Penn, Esquire,
        sonne and heire of Sir William Penn, deceased,
        out of a commendable desire
        to enlarge our English Empire,
        and promote such vseful commodities as may bee
        of benefit to vs and our Dominions,

        'as alsoe to reduce the Savage Natives by
        gentle and iust manners
        to the love of civill Societie
        and Christian Religion
        hath humbley besought leave of vs
        to transport an ample Colonie
        vnto a certaine Countrey
        hereinafter described in the partes of America not yet
            cultivated and planted'

                        that relieves
    Lucky Charles of this nuisance, his debt;

And relieves, by an exodus over the seas
    Of Dissenters, at their own expense—

The land being hilly, 'I would call it New Wales,'
said Penn whose name in Welsh means *a hill.*
But the King's Secretary, from Wales as well,
demurs that such a folly as this Quaker plans
might slight his country's name. Then,
his deep woods in mind, Penn proposes
—Latin scholar, he—'Sylvania.' To this
the King prefixes 'PENN,'
which Penn the Quaker must accept, the name
not signifying vanity in him

since Charles confers his Patent 'haveing regard
to the memorie and meritts of his late father
in divers services and perticulerly
to his *Conduct, courage,* and *difcretion*
under our deareft brother
James Duke of York in that Signall Batell
and victorie obteyned againft the Dutch
in the yeare One thousand and Six hundred sixtie
        five . . .'

And relieves of Friend William with his hectoring pleas—
    The benefits do look immense!

In delight at this barter, King Charles signs the Charter
    And many folk, not just Friends, follow Penn.
They ship out with thanksgiving to seek a good living
    In a new land, where men will be men.

43

The day will dawn like any
Ordinary day, the trees
Growing slowly darker than the sky,

And birds
Whose notes and colors we will learn to name
In their dewy nets of sound
From the night's depths
Sieve the sun
Till it leaps forth
With clarions of light on cloudy shores

Sending its rippling streams among the houses
Set back from grids of streets,
The grids of streets giving on leafy squares
Where great trees arise,
Their millions of green fingers stroking Heaven
Though rooted in the earth we tread,

And in the houses men and women stir.
Turning toward each other lovingly
Husbands clasp their wives and wives their husbands,
Finding one another comely,
While beside them in their trundle-beds and cradles
The faint breath of babes
Rises and falls,
The beds and cradles floating without movement
In the peaceful harbors
Of protected sleep.

44

These people are under the Frame of the Government. The
  Great Law or Body of Laws is their guide, the Great Law
  the Assembly, meeting in Chester, has passed.

Now everyone worships here as he will! That is the first law of
  this Province—of the Body of Laws, this is Chapter I.

Of the Laws there are many, namely LXI (with additions, by
  1690, to the number CCIII),

'For they weakly err, that think there is no other use of
  government than correction, which is the coarsest part;
  experience tells us the greatest part are the regulation and
  care of many other affairs more soft and daily necessary,'

Writes William Penn, whose Body of Laws will regulate Fences
  and Ferries, Weirs, Taverns, Prisons, the Prices of Corn;

Will provide for the Poor; prescribe all Weights & Measures;
  proscribe the willful firing of another's house or barn,
  swearing, and the Defiling of the marriage bed.

The Body of Laws makes challenging another to fight a crime,
  and Whosoever shall introduce into this Province such rude
  and riotous sports and practices

As Prizes, Stage-Plays, Masques, Revels, Bull-baiting,
  Cock-fighting, and the like, shall suffer ten days' hard labour
  or forfeit a fine of twenty shillings.

And whereas Divers persons, as English, Dutch, Swedes, &c.,
have been wont to sell to the Indians, rum and Brandy,
though they know the said Indians are not able to govern
themselves in the use thereof,

Whereby they make the poor natives worse, and not better for
their coming among them, which is a heinous offence to
God and a reproach to the blessed name of Christ and his
holy Religion,

It is therefore Enacted that if anyone shall offend therein, the
person Convicted thereof shall, for each offence, pay five
pounds.

And *Be it Enacted &c.* That if any Indian shall commit any
trespass or Damage against the person or Estate of any
inhabitant of this Province,

Notice shall be given to the king of the Indians that the offender
be brought to his triall,

And shall be tryed by six of the freemen of ye same County
where the Abuse was Committed, and six of the Indians
that are Nearest to that place.

And if any Person in this Province shall at any time herafter
Committ or do any Damage or injury to any Indian,

The matter shall be tryed by six of the freemen of this Province,
and six of the same Indians;

And the king to whom such Indians doth belong shall have
notice thereof, that he may be present and see Justice done
on both sides.

And *Be it enacted &c.* that if any person within this Province (Indians only excepted) shall kill a dog-wolf, hee shall have ten shillings, and if a bitch-wolf, fifteen shillings, to be paid out of the public stock;

Provided such persons brings the wolf's head to one of the Justices of the Peace of that County; Who is to cause the Ears and tongue of the wolf to be cut off;

And if any Indian shall kill a woolf and bring the head and body to a Justice of the peace, hee shall have five shillings, and the skin for his pains.

45

'Governments, like clocks, go from the motion men give them,
and as governments are made and moved by men,
so by them they are ruined too.'

(William Penn is writing
The Frame of the Laws.)

'Wherefore governments rather depend upon men
than men on governments.
Let men be good, and the government cannot be bad.

'If it be ill,
they will cure it.

'But if men be bad, let the government
be never so good, they will endeavour
to warp and spoil it to their turn.

'I know some say, Let us have good laws,
and no matter for the men who execute them.
But let them consider

'that though good laws do well, good men
do better. Good men will never
want good laws, nor suffer ill ones.'

(How capable of perfection, or near it,
by God's grace, is man!)

Of such are the kingdom of this world. Let us rejoice,
There is 'That of God' in each of them.
Of such are the kingdom.

46

I sailed from Deal the tenth of June with four men servants, two maid servants, two children and one boy. We had the whole way over contrary winds, and never favorable for twelve hours together, many tempests and thunderstorms, also the foremast broke twice, so that it was ten weeks before we arrived here. I now from my own experience understand what David says in the 107th Psalm, that on the sea one may perceive not only the wonderful works of God, but also the spirit of the storm.

On our ship no one died and no one was born. Almost all the passengers were seasick for some days, I however for not more than four hours. On the other hand I underwent other accidents, namely, that the two carved lugs over the ship's bell fell right on my back, and during a storm in the night I fell so severely that for some days I had to keep to my bed. These two falls reminded me forcibly of the first fall of our original parents in Paradise, which has come down upon all their posterity, and also of those many falls which I have undergone in this vale of the misery of my exile. *Per varios casus*, etc.

But praised be the fatherly hand of the divine mercy which lifts us up again so many times and holds us back that we fall not entirely into the abyss of the evil one. Georg Wertmüller also fell down extremely hard, Thomas Gasper had an eruption of the body, the English maid had erysipelas, and Isaac Dilbreck, who according to outward appearance was the strongest, succumbed for the greatest length of time. One of the boatmen became insane and our ship was shaken by repeated assaults of a whale.

My company consisted of many sorts. There was a doctor of
medicine with his wife and eight children, a French captain,
a Low Dutch cake-baker, an apothecary, a mason, a smith, a
wheelwright, etc., in all about eighty persons besides the
crew. They were of such different religions and behaviors
that I might not unfittingly compare the ship with Noah's
Ark. In my household I have those who hold to the Roman,
the Lutheran, the Calvinistic, the Anabaptist, and the
Anglican church, and only one Quaker.

On the 20th we sailed past Neu Castle, Upland and Tinicum
and arrived at evening, praise God, safely at Philadelphia;
where on the following day I delivered to William Penn
the letters that I had, and was received by him with amiable
friendliness; of that very worthy man and famous ruler
I might properly write many things;

but my pen—though it is from an eagle, which a so-called
savage lately brought to my house—is much too weak to
express the high virtue of this Christian, for such he is
indeed. He often invites me to his table and has me walk
and ride in his always edifying company.

He heartily loves the Germans and once said openly in my
presence to his councillors and those who were about him, I
love the Germans and desire that you also should love them.
I can at present say no more than that William Penn is a
man who honors God and is honored by Him, who loves
what is good and is rightly beloved by all good men.

Philadelphia
May 30, 1698

I received in proper condition on April 25th, my honored
father's latest, of August 15th, and I was greatly rejoiced by
the sight of his dear handwriting. But to answer his
questions, I would wish that my pen could reach down to
the uttermost depth of my soul, for so should I do the same
with more satisfaction than is now the case.

What form of government have the so-called savages and
half-naked people? Whether they become citizens and
intermarry with the Christians? Again, whether their
children also associate with the Christian children and they
play with one another?

I have found them reasonable people and capable of
understanding good teaching and manners, who give
evidence of an inward devotion to God, and in fact show
themselves much more desirous of a knowledge of God
than are many with you who teach Christianity by words
from the pulpit, but belie the same through their ungodly
lives, and therefore, in yonder great Day of Judgment, will
be put to shame by these heathen.

They believe that there is one God, and the souls of men are
immortal, and that God holds back the Devil from doing
injury to human beings; they say that God dwells in the
most glorious southern land, to which they also shall attain
at some future time, after death. They punish all their
crimes by fines, even murder, and when one kills a woman
he must give double the penalty, because the woman brings
forth children.

We Christians in Germantown and Philadelphia have no longer
the opportunity to associate with them, since their savage
kings have accepted a sum of money from William Penn,
and, together with their people, have withdrawn very far
from us, into the wild forest, where, after their hereditary
custom, they support themselves by the chase, shooting
birds and game and catching fish, and dwell only in huts
made of bushes and trees drawn together. They exchange
their elk and deer-skins, beaver, marten, and turkeys, for
powder, lead, blankets, and brandy, together with other
sweet drinks.

47

Now, out of the darkness
In the twelfth night of the Gamwing
Comes Nutimus, far seer:

He steps upon the Great White Path and pauses,
Shaking, gently shaking
His rattles in the shell of tortoise,
And he sings,

> *Heh!*
> This life that you are living,
> This life—is it real?
> Here, I bring to you
> What the Manito
> Showed me in my dream.

Nutimus takes four steps
Near Grandfather Fire.
Now the drummers cease.
The tribe is gathered, glinting
In feathered robes and flints.
Now the world is silent
In the Big House on this last
Twelfth Night of the Gamwing.

Lenape, says Nutimus, in whose language Lenape
Means The People in the Beginning,
I speak now of a time when I was young,
Time when my father cast me from his fire
To wander in the forest. Fasting,
Not knowing why or where or what to do, I wandered
Weak with sleeplessness, with hunger, waiting

To be told,
To be told by voices or a voice
I had not yet heard,
Had never heard.

Then in that night of hunger,
Night of loneness and confusion,
Night of being lost amid the swirling of the cold and silent
    stars
Came a voice,
To me a voice then came out of my sufferings, saying,

> *Heh!*
> This life that you are living,
> This life—is it real?
> Here, I give you knowledge
> Of the real: This life
> And the After-life.
> Take my blessing, gift
> To all the Lenape.

Nutimus takes four steps advancing
Around the sacred fire, dancing,
Shaking the rattles in his tortoise-shell,
Shaking sacred time.

What is this voice that comforts me? I cried into the
    darkness
Whose is the blessing comforts me, unworthy of his
    blessing?
Who gives this blessing to the Lenape, my people?
And the darkness then began to swirl apart
Back, back toward a far horizon. I could see
The roads that cross, on which my feet must travel, trying
To choose the Great White Path that leads us
Toward the Mountain.
It was the Mountain spoke to me,
It was the Mountain, saying,

Take my blessing, gift
To all the Lenape!

Mountain my Manito raised up his head and spoke,
Mountain the great humped shell of Grandfather
On whose back arose the Earth Our Mother
From the darkness
Of the waters long ago.

Here, said Grandfather,
This life is yours
Where you seek the pure White Path, our fathers',
The Great Spirits' Road. Here
Your life is, where
He Who Owns the Game protects
The Lenape from hunger. Here
In your life is the crossing of the Path
By the forks that lead you
Otherwhere than on
The Sacred Way.

Says Nutimus, his tortoise
Rattles shaking sacred time:

Here, said Grandfather Voice,
Beware
The Crossing paths that lead away from We-elhik,
        the virtues:
Your spirit must be ever humble
Since all you have is given you
By spirit forces, Manitos.
Be grateful for their blessings, pray
For their bestowal. Let
Many voices pray as one.
In your cantico a fine appearance
And dignity will please the Manitos,
Said Grandfather Voice. Be good to other
Men and Women, to the sick, the old.

Value welangosawaken,
Peacefulness, above all things.
Seek blessedness for all who live,
Whatever race, whatever council fire is theirs.

Says Nutimus and sings, advancing
Around Grandfather Fire, dancing,
Shaking rattles in his tortoise-shell,
Shaking sacred time.

Grandfather Voice then called me onward
Says Nutimus, now singing,
Voice of Manito urged me on
Into the darkened sky, the home of
Lightning flashing in its ecstasy of anger
Streaking fiery arrows to the ground.
Fire that leaps into its own mouth, ravenous
To blast itself in frenzy.
Smoke-in-the-Clouds this place, breathing
Pillar of blackness, greyness, choking
White across the lower layers of sky.
And the Voice sang to me, to Nutimus,

> *Heh!*
> This life that you are living,
> This life, is it real?
> Here I give to you
> What is real: This life
> And the After-life.
> Take my blessing! Gift
> To all the Lenape,
> This life and After-life
> To all the Lenape!

And Nutimus, advancing
Around Grandfather Fire
Dancing to the throb of drum

Dancing in the glinting light
Tortoise rattles shaking time,
Making come the sacred time,
Stops—

You, said Manito my Grandfather,
Cannot pass here
In this life. But you
Nutimus, I make far seer.
You see afar where none can go.
And I peered beyond that Place of Storms,
There, on the ten-and-second level of the sky
Saw Pemaxting, highest of all ridges,
The furthest place, from where I heard the singing
Of the happy ones.
The ancestors
Dancing in the steps that I am dancing
In spiral steps around this lodgepole,
They, dancing in a dance of light,
A whorl of starlight, countless ancestors
Treading the Spirit Path across the sky and singing:

        Heb!
        We are what is real!
        In the After-life
        We rejoice, we sing
        Until the life we know
        In the world shall end.
        Then when all our Tribe
        Join with us again
        As Spirits here, not men,
        Together then we go
        Beyond this highest ridge
        To Lenape-ehat,
        Lenape-Where-He-Goes
        With the Manito.

So sang Nutimus, again advancing
Around Grandfather Fire, the drummers drumming
While he, dancing, shakes his tortoise shell,
Makes his rattle shake the sacred time,
Makes his rattle
Stop.

Drummers stop. Grandfather Fire
Blinks in silence.
Silence on the floor of the Big House,
Hushed are the wild creatures of The Spirit Who Owns
    the Game,
Hushed the streams, and quiet
The rocks beside the streams.
The Lenape, like all of them, unspeaking.
The Spirit guardians whose masks hang on the posts, silent,
The four walls, hushed,
Silent the far quarters of the world.

The sacred time is nearly over. Nutimus
Takes each drummer by the hand,
The Bringer-In calls for the wooden bowl of wampum
And to each person gives three equal wampum-beads.
To the drummers, a wampum belt of shoulder length.
The Woman Attendant passes then the bowl of bark
Filled with bloodroot and with paint,
Annointing each with the black paint of the dead,
With red paint of the living.
And now, says Nutimus, my kindred,
As we go out to face the East and pray
Let each, with the unused wampum in his heart
Lift his prayer to the highest level of the sky,
To the dwelling place of the Great Spirit
Our Father
Who made the world.

48

Reader, what I have here written, is not a Fiction, Flam, Whim, or any sinister Design, either to impose upon the Ignorant or Credulous, or to curry Favour with the Rich and Mighty,

but in meer Pity and pure Compassion to the Numbers of Poor Labouring Men, Women, and Children in England, half-starv'd, visible in their meagre looks, that are continually wandering up and down

looking for Employment without finding any, who here need not lie idle a moment, nor want Encouragement or Reward for their Work,

much less Vagabond or Drone it about. Here are no Beggars to be seen.

Jealousie among Men is here very rare, and Barrenness among Women

hardly to be heard of, nor are old Maids to be met with;

for all commonly Marry before they are Twenty,

and seldom any young Married Woman but hath a Child in her Belly, or one upon her lap.

What I have deliver'd concerning this Province, is indisputably true,

I was an Eye-Witness to it all, for I went in the first Ship that was bound from England for that Countrey, since it received the Name of Pensilvania,

which was in the Year 1681. The Ship's Name was the *John and Sarah* of London, Henry Smith Commander. I have declin'd giving any Account of several things which I have only heard others speak of, because I did not see them my self, for I never held that way infallible, to make Reports from Hear-say.

I saw the first Cellar when it was digging for the use of our Governour Will. Penn.

I must needs say, even the present Encouragements are very great and inviting,

for Poor People (both Men and Women) of all kinds can here get three times the Wages for their Labour they can in England or Wales.

I shall instance in a few, which may serve; nay, and will hold in all the rest.

The first was a Black-Smith (my next Neighbour), who himself and one Negro Man he had, got Fifty Shillings in one Day,

by working up a Hundred Pound Weight of Iron, which at Six Pence per Pound (and that is the common Price in that Countrey)

amounts to that Summ.

Labouring-Men have commonly here, between 14 and 15 Pounds a Year,

and their Meat, Drink, Washing, and Lodging; and by the Day

their Wages is generally between Eighteen Pence and Half a Crown, and Diet also;

But in Harvest they have usually between Three and Four Shillings each Day, and Diet.

The Maid Servants Wages is commonly betwixt Six and Ten Pounds per Annum, with very good Accomodation.

And for the Women who get their Livelihood by their own Industry, their Labour is very dear, for I can buy in London a Cheese-Cake for Two Pence, bigger than theirs at that price when at the same time their Milk is as cheap as we can buy it in London,

and their Flour is cheaper by half.

And for Carpenters, both House and Ship, Brick-layers, Masons, either of these Trades-Men will get between Five and Six Shillings every Day constantly.

As to Journey-Men Shooe-Makers, they have Two Shillings per Pair both for Men and Womens Shooes:

And Journey-Men Taylors have Twelve Shillings per Week and their Diet.

Sawyers get betwen Six and Seven Hundred Shillings the Hundred for Cutting of Pine-Boards.

And for Weavers, they have Ten or Twelve Pence the Yard for Weaving of that

which is little more than half a Yard in breadth. Wooll-Combers

have for combing Twelve Pence per Pound. Potters have Sixteen Pence

for an Earthen Pot which may be bought in England for Four Pence.

Tanners may buy their Hides green for Three Half Pence per Pound,

and sell their Leather for Twelve Pence per Pound. And Curriers

have Three Shillings and Four Pence per Hide for Dressing it; they buy their Oyl

at Twenty Pence per Gallon. Brick-Makers have Twenty

Shillings per Thousand for their Bricks at the Kiln.

Felt-Makers will have for their Hats Seven Shillings a piece,

such as may be bought in England for Two Shillings; yet they buy their Wooll

commonly for Twelve or Fifteen Pence per Pound. And as to Glaziers,

they will have Five Pence a Quarry for their Glass.

The Butchers for killing a Beast, have Five Shillings and their Diet; and they may buy a good fat cow for Three Pounds.

The Brewers sell such Beer as is equal in Strength to that in London, half Ale and half Stout for Fifteen Shillings per barrel;

and their Beer is in more esteem than English Beer in Barbadoes, and is sold for a higher Price there.

And for Silver-Smiths, they have between Half a Crown and Three Shillings an Ounce for working their Silver, and for Gold equivalent.

Last-Makers have Sixteen Shillings per dozen for their Lasts.

And Heel-Makers have Two Shillings a dozen for their Heels.

Wheel and Mill-Wrights, Joyners, Brasiers,

Pewterers, Dyers, Fullers, Comb-Makers,

Wyer-Drawers, Cage-Makers,

Card-Makers, Painters,

Cutlers,

Rope Makers,

Carvers,

Block-Makers,

Turners,

Button-Makers,

Hair and Wood Sieve-Makers,

Bodies-Makers, Gun-Smiths,

Lock-Smiths, Nailers,

File-Cutters,

Skinners,

Furriers,

Glovers,

Pattern-Makers, Watch-Makers, Clock-Makers,

Sadlers,

Coller-Makers,

Barbers,

Printers,

Book-Binders, and

all other Trades-Men, their Gains and Wages

are about the same proportion as the forementioned Trades in
their Advancements, as to what they have in England.

Of Lawyers and Physicians

I shall say nothing,

because this Country is very Peaceable and Healthy; long may it
so continue

and never have occasion for the Tongue of the one, nor the Pen
of the other.

And now for their Lots and Lands in City and Countrey, in their great Advancement since they were first laid out, that which might have been bought for Fifteen Shillings is now sold for Fourscore Pounds in ready silver;

and likewise some Land that Lies near the City, that Sixteen Years ago might have been Purchas'd for Six or Eight Pounds the Hundred Acres, cannot now be bought under One Hundred and Fifty, or Two Hundred Pounds.

However there still remain Lots of Land both in the aforesaid City and Countrey, that any may Purchase almost as cheap as they could at the first Laying out or Parcelling of either City or Country;

which is the likeliest to turn to account to those that lay their Money out upon it, and in a shorter time than the aforementioned Lots and Lands that are already improved, and for several Reasons.

In the first place, the Countrey is now well inhabited by the Christians, who have great Stocks of all sorts of Cattle that encrease extraordinarily,

and upon that account they are oblig'd to go farther up into the Countrey, because there is the chiefest and best place for their Stocks, and they get the richest Land, for the best lies thereabouts.

Secondly, Farther into the Countrey is the Principal Place to Trade with the Indians for all sorts of Pelts, as Skins and Furs, and also Fat Venison, of whom People may Purchase cheaper by three Parts in four than they can at the City of Philadelphia.

Thirdly, Backwards from the Countrey lies the Mines where is Copper and Iron, besides other Metals and Minerals, of which there is some Improvement made already in order to bring them to greater Perfection; and that will be a means to erect more Inland Market-Towns, which exceedingly promote Traffick.

Fourthly, and lastly, Because the Countrey at first laying-out, was void of Inhabitants (excepting the Heathens, or very few Christians not worth naming)

and not many People caring to abandon a quiet and easie life in their Native Countrey to seek out a hazardous and careful one in a Foreign Wilderness or Desert Countrey, even to arrive at which they must pass over a vast Ocean, expos'd to some Dangers, and not a few Inconveniences:

But now all those Cares, Fears and Hazards are vanished, for the Countrey is pretty well Peopled, and very much Improv'd, and will be more every Day,

now the Dove is return'd with the Olive-branch of Peace in her Mouth.

49

The Dove is returned with the Olive-branch of Peace in her
    Mouth
And the Branch of Jesse, the grape, is also planted.

A great people are gathered beside a river.

This is a green and country Town
Where History begins anew.
Here the mistakes of the past and the sufferings of the past are
    cleansed and washed away.
Here none need ever suffer to prove his faith.
Here faith, work, and love for one another
Will bless the settlers of this pleasant land.

Here the woman, awaking, will set the fire for her husband's
    breakfast,
Her husband will feed the cattle and bring the stove wood in,
    then sit to the breakfast she has made,
and later, he'll plough, or reap, or load his waggon with corn
And sell, and buy, and meet with his near neighbors.
They will set awhile in the shade of a tall tree at the crossroads
And consider the issues, and weigh the alternatives
And come, in concert, to wise and mutual consent.

Now the Proprietor fits his manse at Pennsbury with glass
    windowpanes.
He sends to London for highboys, silver salvers, tasselled
    canopies to deck his Barge of State.
Hannah his wife counts pewter spoons, her tankards, linen
    towels and sheets with lacy edgings.
His servants trim the boxwood on the garden walks.

In the kitchen his cooks turn spitted venison.
They set the johnny-cake a-cooling on the trenchers.
Twenty sachems have pitched their wigwams on Pennsbury
    meadow.
The feast will be ready for them in time.

Listen—the sounds of work in the kitchen, work in the garden,
Work of the blacks harvesting corn in Penn's broad fields
Are, for a moment, charmed to silence
By the spell
Of laughter—
Penn's baby boy is in his mother's arms in the garden.
This infant gurgling now with innocent laughter as his mother
    dandles him in her arms,
He will be Proprietor one day.
He will inherit Pennsbury, Barge, highboys, salvers, his father's
    title and rights and duties.
His cooks some day will spit the venison for the visiting Lenape
    chieftains and their braves.

And now, in the outlands, certain settlers in the hot summer
    stillness toil,
To fell trees, clear stumps, build and daub their rude log houses,
    plough the uncut tangled roots and coax
A little corn from this savage alien soil.
Penn has said, 'I have put the power in the people.'
These are some of the people
In whom he has put the power.

This one swigs a noggin of rum and looks at the clearing
Cleared by nobody's toil but his,
His was the axe, the arm that swung it, his,
The back that strained against the tree-stump was his back,
The hand that notched and set the logs his own.
This is the cabin that he has built, and by the door
Stands his own wife, stirring the fire in the outside kitchen.

There's his child crawling about the earthen floor.
He is beholden to no one.
His gun is over the doorsill.

He'd as like run the tax-collector back to Philadelphia with
        a ramrod up his ass
As shoot an Indian in the heel to watch him dance.

If anyone's son is going to govern this province some day
Why not his before somebody else's?

Indians laden with skins of otter, skins of deer
Glide warily past. They are on their way now
To sell their season's hunting in Philadelphia.

He who planted pumpion and corn is now a hunter.
He who carved masks for the Canteco hunts also.
The arrow-chipper now has no apprentices,
No young man tests the sapling ash to make new bows.
Now the Lenape hunt with boughten flintlocks,
Hunt more deer than ever they have eaten,
Hunt the otter, which they never ate.
All the Lenape are huntsmen now,
So gentlemen at court may doff their hats of fur, of otter
That lately swam the Susquehanna, the Neshaminy.
Bundles of skins they bring to Philadelphia.
There merchants buy cheap. They sell dear, in London.

Everyone concerned cuts a nick of the silver.

In the woods some settlers watch them stagger homeward.
They have exchanged their season's hunting for some silver,
Exchanged their silver for more rum.
Some will sell their lands for rum,
Pass their birthright through their guts, then roam
To hunt more skins on the hunting-grounds of others.
Certain settlers think, Ain't it a shame these Indians

Have to carry skins to Philadelphia
When they could trade them and get drunk right here?
Penn has laws against selling rum to Indians
But some, unlicensed, bring, on horse-drawn waggons,
Puncheons of rum to their own clearings.

They drive a good trade, buying very cheap. Their rum is dear.

Still deeper in the woods, west of the Susquehannah
Is the wilderness
Eden. No
Peace there now. Lord Baltimore contests
Penn's Royal Patent with his own, drawn by a king
Who'd never seen this country—no one at court
Had seen this country. Charles,
In all things profligate, may have twice given
The same wilderness—

Penn's settlers cross the Susquehannah
But ruffians from Annapolis by night
Break down their corncrakes, barns, their very doors.
Thomas Creasap and his bloody-minded gang
Defy the magistrates at Lancaster.
The scent of blood
Hangs in the still air of the Western wood.

When Puritan Plato made up his good R E P U B L I C,
when lordly Harington his O C E A N A conceived,
Was either plagued by boundary claims?
Were citizens in those Commonwealths loath to pay
Their just dues, or grant to their Proprietors
Privileges the law reserves
In his name, and in his children's names?

This Province's laws being under the laws of England,
Penn must return once more to Court,

Must plead again to the King for justice,
Plead for guarantees
For his Province,
For his People, to whom

From his ship in the River Delaware
He bids farewell:

50

'AND THOU PHILADELPHIA

'the virgin settlement of this Province
    named before thou wert born   what love
        what care   what service   and what travail

'have there been to bring thee forth
    and preserve thee
        from such as would abuse and defile thee.

'O that thou mayest be kept from the evil
    that would overwhelm thee
        that faithful to the God of thy mercies

'in the life of righteousness
    thou mayest be preserved
        to the end.

'My soul prays to God for thee
    that thou mayest stand
        in the days of trial

'that thy children may be blest of the Lord
    and thy people saved
        by His power.'

51

The sachems who used to leap with Miquon are gone now.
No longer do they feast at Canteco and sing.

> 'Guillaume Penn founded the town of Philadelphia
> which is today a bustling, busy city.
> He began by making alliances with his neighbors
>   the Indians.

Tamamend and Idquayhon and Tomackhickon on moonless
    nights
Now dance along the Spirit Path. Their sisters' sons
    succeed them.

> 'This is the only treaty between these people
> and the Christians which has neither
> been sworn, nor broken.

How many suns have risen, moons have set
Since Miquon in his great canoe sailed home.

> 'The natives, instead of fleeing
> into the forest, accepted the presence
> of the peaceful Quakers.

They come to Philadelphia to renew the claim
Of friendship, as in olden times.

> 'They loved these newcomers in the same degree
> that they abhorred the other Christians,
> who conquered and destroyed them.

Penn's Governor receives the sachems now. They speak
Of their friend Miquon, give again their pledge of Peace:

> 'Charmed by the gentleness of their neighbors,
> before long these so-called savages
> came in a body

In strings upon the white man's table they lay down
The unspent wampum of their hearts.

> 'to request of Guillaume Penn that he
> include them, too, among his subjects.
> This was something new to behold—

With ceremonious words the Governor replies,
Gives assurances, and ceremonial gifts:

> 'a sovereign familiarly addressed
> —you could speak to him without lifting your hat!—
> a government without priests,

50 Duffels, 20 Blanketts, 12 Doz. Pr. of Shooes,
30 Hose, 6 Doz. Knives, 1 Dozen Buckles,

> 'a people without an army, all the citizens
> equal, their magistrates living among them,
> dwelling without envy together.

Chiefs and Indians all give solemn thanks. Then they depart
To their shrunken hunting-grounds.

> 'Guillaume Penn could well have boasted
> he had brought forth on earth the fabled
> Age of Gold. What's more likely is,

At dawn the dewy valley air is tinged now
With smoke from new chimneys, new fires;

      'it never existed at all—except
      in Pennsylvania! I tell you,
      I myself love the Quakers—

The deer, seeking the thicket where it lay,
Pauses, puzzled, in the raw new clearing.

      'yes, and except sea travel makes me sick,
      I would complete my span of days
      contentedly, O Pennsylvania,

The swamp behind the beaver-dam is dry.
The dam is pulled apart, gone is the beaver.

      'upon your breast. Ma chère
      Madame, je suis à vous en prose et vers
      avec le plus tendre dévouement—
                       Voltaire.'

52

They have forgiven me, the Grandfathers,
Seeing everything and knowing all.

I have danced among them, danced the maze
Of steps around the lodgepole of the sky,
Sacred steps that glimmer in the sky,
Free from hunger, free from all desires
As the smoke from scented council fires.

Knowing everything and seeing all,
Though we chant the whole night through
In the rustle of the wind in the branches,
Calling in the riffle of the air that caresses
The leaves, the mosses,
The least grasses,
No one, here, who heeds us
Understands.

The Big House is empty.

Nobody comes to the Gamwing.

To this burial-ground of Friends,
To the tomb of Logan I have come.
I dance on Logan's grave to summon
Logan's spirit from his sleep.
I dance,
I beat this magic drum!

Logan's Ghost:

What, what? O, my distress was but a dream . . .
Seeing him miscatalogue the books

In the Loganian Library, I tried
To tell him he'd misread the Greek—my hand
Touched his shoulder, but he felt nothing . . .
What is this racket that disturbs my rest,
This beat that throbs and thrills beneath my stone?
—Is it Teedyuscung? Sassoonan?
Ah, Nutimus, have you come yet again?
So long after we last spoke together
You invade the silence of my grave.

Spirit of Nutimus:

I come now as I came before
To hear your claim of ancient deeds.
I come now as I came before
This time to undo what was done.
I deny the claim that Miquon's son
Made then
And you, Friend Logan, made.

Logan's Ghost:

Governor Thomas Penn showed you the deed
Of 1686 your forebears made,
Deeding The Forks to William Penn.
Go back, Nutimus, to wherever it is your spirit
Finds its rest. We, being dead,
Cannot change History, nor can the living.

Spirit of Nutimus:

Although they have forgiven me,
I cannot rest.
Although we are but shadow-shapes,
Papery ghosts like the night's light-bringer Moon
That thinly floats by day, I would
Undo the evils done
When we spoke at Durham and at Philadelphia,

You and I and Governor Thomas Penn,
Great Miquon's son
With the snake's tongue.

Logan's Ghost:

How could you have known that ancient Bargain?
How keep in mind how much of the land was sold
Half a century ago, when you
Were but a babe in arms, you
Who have no writings?

Spirit of Nutimus:

I remember what my Father told.
We do not need to scratch black marks on paper
To remember how we sell our land.
He who holds the land holds what is bounded
By certain Rivers, Creeks, and Mountains.
It is not his alone—the land is shared
With many families. He must consult them.
And when he sells, it is with them he shares
The duffels, coats, shirts, the hoes and axes,
The pairs of stockings and the bars of lead,
The fish hooks and the awls he shares
And tells them for which lands the goods were given him.
Besides, the Chief who sells calls in still others,
Chiefs from elsewhere to be witnesses,
And to them, too, he gives a share
So that they may well remember.
Our fathers tell their sons, and we remember.
And this we think a better way than yours,
For when you have a Writing for the Land
From us, you lock it in a chest so no one knows
Which lands you bought, or what you paid for them.
And then you sell our Land in little pieces,
You get so rich that you can build
Houses that jut into the sky, while we,

Having little and dividing that among our friends,
Must live in wigwams. Yet we never
Claim any land we ever fairly sold
To which we know we have no right.

Logan's Ghost:

Old Nutimus, how had you any right
To lands on the Delaware's West Bank?
Everybody knows that you were born
Not at the Forks, but on the Eastern side.
Not at the Forks—you were born in Jersey.

Spirit of Nutimus:

My right to these Lands at the Forks
Came into the world with me
From my mother's womb. These were her lands.
The River is no boundary to us,
Indians of the same Nation
Live on either side.
But then, Friend Logan, how have *you*
Rights to Land on either side,
For everyone well knows that you were born
In Ireland, which is another country?

Logan's Ghost:

You troublesome fellow, you know that all I claim
Is subject to the Charter and our laws.
My fealty was to our great Proprietor
And to his heirs. I made their interests mine
Under the laws that William Penn devised.
For years the Penns' defense against the people—
All that rabble who would seize the power
The law vests in their true Proprietors—
Was I. I guarded and I guided them
In property, in politics, in war.

To the Founder's sons I was a Nestor. Nutimus,
Since you could not remember that old treaty
Maykerichshe made with William Penn,
His sons Thomas and John in Philadelphia
Showed you the paper, had it read aloud,
And they said,
All of the Indians must be sensible
Of William Penn's great love for them
And of his Justice, for it was his Rule
Neither to take possession, nor let others
To possess themselves of any Lands
Without first purchasing them from the Indians.
Then William Penn's sons met you, Nutimus, in Durham,
They mentioned the old friendship which their Father
Had established with the Indians, and discoursed
About the Lands—

Spirit of Nutimus:

To the Proprietor I gave a Belt of Wampum of four rows
Desiring to preserve his Father's Love.
Let us, I said, avoid misunderstanding.
The Proprietor knows well how run the Lines
As mentioned in the deed.
But we,
We do not fully understand them.

Logan's Ghost:

Yes, and Thomas Penn produced a map
Which, you agreed, showed lines upon the Land
Your ancestors had sold to William Penn.

Spirit of Nutimus:

I agreed, the way a deer
Moves from a favorite thicket when the lynx
Snarls in his path. I agreed,

137

Friend Logan, only after you
Threatened to throw me off my land, and warned
That you would make great logs, great rocks and stones fall
    down
Upon my people's path to Philadelphia,
For you, Friend Logan, were so great a man
As your two arms outstretched could scarcely measure,
While I, you said, was looked upon by you
With the scorn you showed your left hand's littlest finger.

We never heard contempt like that from Miquon.

Logan's Ghost:

From Miquon you, like us, received the treaty
Which you stubbornly would not recall.
I merely urged on you the wiser course.
And so after three years of your palaver
With sachems in the forest, you agreed,
You and Tishekunk, to validate
The old treaty ceding us these lands.
You set your signatures on a new treaty.

Spirit of Nutimus:

Now that with the ancestors I've seen
Everything and know all that we could not know,
I would cut off this hand that signed away
My birthright and my children's
For a false deed
—The treaty Thomas Penn held in his hand
Had *blanks* where should have been the measured lines!
His treaty was a copy only
Of a lost original?—there was
No lost original,
That treaty never was.
And the map he showed us, showed a river
Where we knew Tohiccon Creek to flow

Into the Delaware, and called that Creek
The West Branch of the Delaware
Some twenty miles to northward—thus
Deceiving us.
If this were but the last of his deceits, Friend Logan!
This time, Friend Logan, I care not for your threats,
This time I see beyond the traps and snares
Set for my people by good Miquon's shifty son.
I will not sign, this time, the treaty giving you
My mother's Land, my children's Lands,
The Forks of the Delaware.
O Hand, my Hand, stay still,
Refuse the inked quill,
Be still, be stake, be stone!

Logan's Ghost:

All this, your grief and your supposèd guilt,
All needless, all misunderstood,
And all now futile since you can no more
Unsign this treaty and depopulate
The lands the old chiefs sold to William Penn
Than restore to Priam all his smouldering walls
Or reclaim the lands Bucephalus bestrode.

Spirit of Nutimus:

You speak of sachems I have never known.
This time I will refuse to set my hand and seal
Upon the lies of the young Proprietor,
Thomas Penn.
Hand, O Hand of mine, refuse
To grasp the inked quill!

Logan's Ghost:

It is no use, my friend. We are but given
The one chance of our lives to seize the course

Of history, if choice of ours it is;
We stood there at a crossroad, you and I
And Governor Thomas Penn and Tishekunk;
At that intersection of our wills
One path, a faint trail through the moss-grown forest
Barely perceptible, save to the deer.
The other, a roadway for the ox and waggons
Bringing iron out of the mines at Durham,
Carting thither all the necessaries
Of civilization. None of us can stand
In the way of progress, Nutimus.

Spirit of Nutimus:

What you call progress is your way to wealth,
You who owned the iron mines at Durham
And needed all my trees to burn for charcoal.
My hunting-ground was reaped to feed your furnace.
Hand, O hand of mine, refuse
The quill, the ink, the treaty—

Logan's Ghost:

Nutimus, you see it is impossible.
You see us there in Philadelphia convened.
There is Barefoot Brunston, your Interpreter.
You hear him read the Treaty, first in English,
Then translated in your Indian tongue.
History must have its way with us.
We hear the Treaty yet again. You cannot
Change a comma, or erase your name:

53

WE, TEESHAKOMEN, alias TISHEEKUNK, AND NOOTAMIS,
alias NUTIMUS, two of the Sachema's or Chiefs
of the Delaware Indians,
having, almost three years ago, at Durham,
begun a Treaty
with our honourable Brethren John and Thomas Penn,
at which Treaty Several Deeds were produced and Shewed to us
by our Said Brethren,
concerning several Tracts of Land which our Fforefathers
had, more than Fifty Years ago,
Bargained and Sold unto our good Ffriend and Brother
William Penn,
the Ffather of said John and Thomas Penn,
and in particular

One Deed from Maykeerickkishsho, Sayhoppy and
    Taughhaughsey,
the Chiefs or Kings of the Northern Indians on the Delaware,
who, for large Quantities of Goods delivered by the Agents
of William Penn to those Indian Chiefs,

did Bargain and Sell unto the said William Penn
all those Tract or Tracts of Land lying
and being in the Province of Pennsylvania
beginning

upon a line formerly laid out from a Corner
Spruce Tree, by the River Delaware,
About Makeerickckitton, and from thence
running along the ledge or foot
of the Mountains, West North West,
to a corner White Oak marked

with the Letter
P,
Standing

by the Indian Path that leadeth
to an Indian Town called Playwickey,
and from thence extending
Westward to Neshameney Creek,
from which said line the said Tract or Tracts
thereby Granted, doth extend itself
Back into the Woods

As far as Man can goe
in one day and a half,

And bounded on the Westerly Side with the Creek called
        Neshameney,
or the most Westerly branch thereof, So far as the said Branch
        doth extend,
And from thence by line   to the utmost extend
Of the said one day and a half's Journey,
And from thence   to the aforesaid
River Delaware,
and from thence down the Several courses of the said River
to the first mentioned Spruce Tree.

We have, after more than two Years since the Treaty at
        Pennsbury
now come to Philadelphia, together with our chief Sachems
Monockyhickon, and several of our Old Men,
And upon a further Treaty held upon the same Subject,
We Do Acknowledge Ourselves
And every of Us,
To be fully satisfied that the above described Tract or Tracts of
        Land
were truly Granted and Sold by the said Maykeerickkishsho,
Sayhoppy and Taughhaughsey,

Unto the said William Penn
and his Heirs,

and for a further Confirmation thereof,
We, the said Tishekunk, and Nutimus, Do,
For ourselves and all other Delaware Indians
Fully, clearly,
and Absolutely
Remise, Release, and forever Quit claim
unto the same John Penn, Thomas Penn, and Richard Penn,

all our Right,
Title,
Interest, and pretensions whatsoever
of, in, or to the said Tract or Tracts of Land
and every Part and Parcel thereof,
so that neither We,
or any of us,
or our Children,
shall or may at any time hereafter,
have challenge, Claim, or Demand
any Right or Title,
Interest, or pretensions whatsoever
of, in, or to the said tract or Tracts of Land,
or any Part thereof,
but of and from the same shall be
Excluded, and

Forever Debarred.

And We do hereby further Agree,
that the extent of the said Tract or Tracts of Land
Shall be forthwith
Walked,
Travelled, or gone over
By proper Persons

To be appointed for that Purpose,
According to the directions of the aforementioned Deed.

In Witness Whereof, We
have hereunto set our hands and Seals,
at Philadelphia, the Twenty-fifth day
of the Month called August,
In the Year, According to the English Account,
One thousand Seven hundred and thirty seven,

TEESHACOMIN   His mark

NOOTAMIS   his mark

54

Logan's Ghost:

Is it not as I foretold?
To the ancient treaty you have set
Your hand and seal. You have but done what you
Were meant to do.

Spirit of Nutimus:

'Excluded, and
Forever Debarred'
—My children and my children's children
From my lands, my mother's lands,
The hunting-grounds my ancestors have camped on . . .

What you did then and caused thence to be done
Broke the Chain of Friendship Miquon made.

Logan's Ghost:

We did what's nowise contrary to the law.

Spirit of Nutimus:

'As far as Man can goe
In one day and a half . . .'

Your walker did not walk as Indians walk,
Walk awhile, sit and puff a pipe awhile,
Then walk not run for twenty mile.
Your walker Edward Marshall run run run,
Not stop to shoot a squirrel or take a rest.
Walked too fast for Solomon Jennings.
He quit the walk and stumbled to his farm.

Walked too fast for other walker—
James Yeates went blind and died
From running running running all that time.
He did not walk as Indians walk
Through the forests over roots and thickets,
He follow trail your men had made before him.
Axes cleared the underbrush before he start.
He did not walk as Indians walk.
Indians come along to see the walk was fair,
John Combush and Neepaheilomon.
They wore out moccasins, and in disgust
They quit. They saw this was a cheat.
No man, walking fair, could walk
Sixty-five miles
In one day and half a day
But by a cheat.

Logan's Ghost:

What Governor Penn had done was done according
To the letter of the treaty that you signed.
Of course the thing was done with certain forethought.
Three quarters of a million acres of prime land
Were thus secured for sale by the poor Penns.
Renouncing the austere life of the Meeting,
They had in England lived beyond their means.
Now wed to Lady Juliana Fermor,
Though drawing almost nil from settlers' taxes,
Thomas must ride to Church in coach and four.

Spirit of Nutimus:

They have forgiven me, the ancestors.
They knew I could not know that where my wigwam
Leaned among the moss-encrusted trees
You and Thomas Penn would make your fortunes.
They knew I could not know that you,
Friend Logan, who had come to us with Miquon,

You, whom we thought to be our friend,
Would turn against the Lenape,
Would betray our people to our stronger cousins,
The Six Nations.

Logan's Ghost:

Despite the presents we for years had given you
When your Delawares took gifts from Fort Duquesne,
Becoming allies of our enemies, the French,
As President of the Council of the Province
I had to seek for England stronger friends.

Spirit of Nutimus:

I was King among the Lenape. I had no quarrel
With King George or with King Louis far away.
Why do they not fight near their own wigwams?
Why must the Indians in our woods fight for those kings?
The Chain of Friendship which should hold as long
As Sun and Moon move in the Heavens, broke
When you deceived the Lenape,
Broke when you turned to the Six Nations,
Betrayed my people to their power,
When by your sufferance Canassatego
The Iroquois, who had no claim
To land below the Kittattiny Mountains,
Ordered us from our own grounds—

Canassatego's Shade:

Brethren, the Governor, and Council:

The other Day you informed Us of the Misbehaviour of our
    Cousins the Delawares with respect to their continuing to
    Claim and refusing to remove from some Land on the River
    Delaware,

notwithstanding their Ancestors had sold it by Deed under
their Hands & Seals to the Proprietors for a valuable
Consideration upwards of fifty Years ago,

and notwithstanding that they themselves had about   Years
ago, after a long and full Examination, ratified that Deed of
their Ancestors, and given a fresh one under their Hand
and Seals,—

Spirit of Nutimus:

What do you hear, Friend Logan? What I hear
Is a white man's jointed doll who speaks with tongue
Nursled on an English lawyer's words.

Canassetego's Shade:

—and then you requested Us to remove them, enforcing your
Request with a String of Wampum.

Afterwards you laid on the Table by Conrad Weiser our own
Letters, some of our Cousins' Letters, and the several
Writings to prove the Charge against our Cousins with a
Draught of the Land in Dispute.

We see with our own Eyes

that they have been a very unruly People,

and are altogether wrong in their Dealings with You.

We have concluded to remove them, and Oblige them to go
over the River Delaware, and to quit all Claim to any Lands
on this side for the future, since they have received Pay for
them and it is gone straight through their Guts long ago.

To confirm to You that we will Execute this your Request we
lay down this String of Wampum in return for Yours.

*[Lays down the wampum before James Logan; turns then to
     Nutimus]*

Cousins,

Let this Belt of Wampum serve to Chastize You;
You should be taken by the Hair of the Head and shak'd
     severely till you recover your Senses and become Sober;
you don't know what Ground you stand on, nor what you do.
Our Brother Onas' case is very just and plain,
and his Intentions to preserve ffriendship;
but your Cause, your Cause is bad, your Heart far from being
     upright, and you are maliciously bent to break the Chain of
     ffriendship with our Brother Onas.
We have seen with our own Eyes a Deed
signed by nine of your Ancestors above fifty years ago for this
     very Land and a Release Sign'd not many Years since by
     some of your selves and Chiefs now living.

Spirit of Nutimus:

Forgive me, Ancestors, knowing all.
How could I, then or now, have stayed my hand?

Canassetego's Shade:

But how came you to take upon you to Sell Land at all?
We conquer'd you, we made
Women of you,
you know you are Women, and can no more sell Land than
     Women.
Nor is it fit you should have the Power of Selling Lands
since you would abuse it.
This Land that you Claim
is gone through your Guts.
You have been furnished with Cloathes and Meat and Drink by
     the Goods paid you for it, and now You want it again
Like Children as you are.

149

We find you are none of our Blood,
You Act a dishonest part not only in this but in other Matters.
Your Ears are ever Open to slanderous Reports about our
    Brethren.
You receive them with as much greediness as Lewd Women
    receive the Embraces of Red Men.
And for all these reasons we charge you to remove at once.
We don't give you the liberty to think about it.
You are Women;
take the advice of a Wise Man and remove immediately.
We, therefore, Assign you
two Places to go—
either to Wyomin or Shamokin. You may go to either of these,
and then we shall have you more under our Eye,
and shall see how You behave.
Don't deliberate, but remove away and take this Belt of
    Wampum.

[*Canassatego holds another String of Wampum and adds further*—]

After our just reproof and absolute Order to depart from the
    Land, you are now to take Notice of what we have further
    to say.
This String of Wampum serves to forbid You,
Your Children and Grand Children,
to the latest Posterity,
for ever meddling in Land Affairs,
neither you nor any who shall descend from You, are ever
    hereafter
to presume to sell any land,
for which Purpose you are to Preserve this string in Memory of
    what your Uncles have this Day given you in Charge.
We have some other Business now to transact with our
    Brethren, and therefore, Cousins, depart the Council and
    consider what has been said to you!

Logan's Ghost:

I, who thought to spend Eternity
Conversing with John Locke and Shaftesbury,
Seneca and Marc Aurelius
On the nature of a virtuous life
Am instead awakened by a savage
And must rehearse old treaties, old negotiations,
Must relive the inescapable design
And, knowing all the consequences now,
Still make the same irreparable choices.

Spirit of Nutimus:

> The Sun still climbs
> Out of the Night to warm us,
> Still the Moon
> Is hatched from her dark egg
> To swell, then vanish
> In the morning sky.
> When you took wampum
> From Canassatego
> You broke the Chain
> Of Friendship Miquon made.
> You enter now
> The Place of Storms, where fiery
> Arrows streak
> Across our night, and thunder
> Is but the wrathful
> Echo of my drum.

55

'Whereas, the Delaware tribe of Indians, and others in
Confederacy with them, have for some Time past, without
the least Provocation, and contrary to their most Solemn
Treaties, fallen upon this Province

'and in a most cruel, savage, and perfidious manner, killed and
butchered great Numbers of the Inhabitants, and carried
others into barbarous Captivity; burning and destroying
their Habitations, and laying waste the Country.

> *I admit that there are good white men,*
> *but they bear no proportion to the bad.*

'And Whereas, not withstanding the friendly Remonstrances
made to them by this Government, and the Interposition
and positive Orders of our faithful Friends and Allies the
Six Nations, to whom they owe Obedience and Subjection,

> *The bad must be the strongest,*
> *For they rule.*

'requiring and commanding them to desist from any further
Acts of Hostility against us, and to return to their
Allegiance, and said Indians do still continue their cruel
Murders and Ravages, sparing neither Age nor Sex;

> *They do what they please.*
> *They enslave those who are not of their colour.*

'I have, therefore, by and with the Advice and consent of the Council, thought fit to issue this Proclamation; and do hereby declare the said Delaware Indians, and all others who, in Conjunction with them, have committed Hostilities against His Majesty's Subjects within this Province, to be Enemies, Rebels, and Traitors to his Most Sacred Majesty;

> *They would make slaves of us if they could,*
> *but as they cannot do it,*

'I do hereby require all his Majesty's Subjects of this Province, and earnestly invite those of the neighbouring Provinces, to embrace all Opportunities of pursuing, taking, killing, and destroying said Delaware Indians and all others confederated with them in committing hostilities, Incursions, Murders, or Ravages upon this Province.

> *they kill us!*
> *There is no faith to be placed in their words.*

'I do hereby declare and promise, that there shall be paid out of Sixty Thousand Pounds to all and every Person and Persons, as well Indians as Christians not in the Pay of the Province, the several and respective Premiums and Bounties following, that is to say:

> *They are not like the Indians, who are enemies only*
> *while at war, and are friends in peace.*

'For every Male Indian Enemy above Twelve Years Old who shall be taken Prisoner and deliver'd at any Forts garrisoned by the Troops in the Pay of the Province, or at any of the County Towns to the Keepers of the common Jails there, the Sum of One Hundred and Fifty Spanish Dollars or Pieces of Eight;

They will say to an Indian,
'My friend! My brother!'

'For the scalp of every Male Indian Enemy above the age of
Twelve, produced as Evidence of their being killed, the sum
of One Hundred and Thirty Pieces of Eight;

They will take him by the hand
and at that same moment destroy him.

'For every Female Indian taken Prisoner and brought in as
aforesaid, and for every Male Indian Prisoner under the Age
of Twelve taken Prisoner and brought in as aforesaid, One
Hundred and Thirty Pieces of Eight;

'For the Scalp of every Indian Woman, produced as Evidence of
their being killed, the Sum of Fifty Pieces of Eight;

And so you will also be treated by them before long.
Remember!

'And for every English Subject that has been taken and carried
from this Province into Captivity that shall be recovered
and brought in and delivered at the City of Philadelphia to
the Governor of the Province, the sum of One Hundred
and Fifty Pieces of Eight,

'but nothing for their Scalps;

'And that there shall be paid to every Officer or Soldier as are or
shall be in the Pay of the Province who shall redeem and
deliver any English Subject carried into Captivity as
aforesaid, or shall take, bring in, and produce any Enemy
Prisoner, or Scalp as aforesaid,

'one-half of the said several and respective Premiums and
Bounties.

This day I have warned you
to beware of such friends as these.

'Given under my Hand and the Great Seal of the Province at
 Philadelphia, the Fourteenth Day of April, in the
 Twenty-Ninth Year of His Majesty's Reign, and in the
 Year of Our Lord One Thousand Seven Hundred and Fifty
 Six.

'Robt. H. Morris,
Deputy Governor.'

I know the long knives.
They are not to be trusted.

Pachgantschilas,
War Chief of the Delawares.

56

Halas, halas! we know now who they are, these white men who
    came out of the Sea
To rob us of our land. With smiles they came, but soon
Turned into Snakes or foes.

The Wallam Olum was set down by Lekhibit, the Writer,
Set down to keep in mind our glory.
Shall I write another to record our fall?
No, our enemies have written that, but I shall speak
Of what they do not know or what conceal.

We have had many kings since the Yankwis called the English
    came
With Mikwon and his friends.
All were well received, we fed Corn to all,
Let them live with us, build houses, plant Corn
As our friends, our allies, because they were hungry.
We thought they were children of Sunland, not Snakes
Or children of Snakes.

And they were traders. Fine new tools they brought
And weapons and cloths and beads.
We gave them our skins and our wampum for these,
And we liked them, liked their things
Because we thought they were good, being made
By children of Sunland.

But alas they brought with them Fireguns & Fire Water also
Which burned & killed. And after Mikwon
Came the children of King George, Dolojo Sachema
Who said more land, more land, we must have

More land, and no bounds could we put
To their steps, their increase.

In the North were our good friends the children of King Louis,
Allies of our allies, of our enemies the foes,
Children of Lowi Sachema. Yet Dolojo
Always wanted war with them.

Netwatwees became king of all the Nations in the West
At Ohio on the River Cayahaga with the Hurons, our old allies,
And he calls all from the East.

But in the East was Teedyuscung king at Mahoning,
Teedyuscung bribed by the Yankwis; there in his own house
He was burnt and many of our people massacred at
      Lancaster   [1762]
By the Land robber Yankwis.

Then we joined our friend Lowi in a war against the Yankwis.
But they were strong, they took Northland from Lowi
And came to us in Ohio when peace was made.
We called them Kichikani, Big Knives.

Then Whiteyes and Killbuck were chiefs and all the nations
      near us
Were allies under us or under our grandchildren.
When the Eastern fires resisted Dolojo
They said we should be another fire with them,
But on Muskingum they killed our Turtle chiefs and brothers
And Hopokan of the Wolf Tribe was king.
He made war on the Kichikani Yankwis, chose Dolojo for ally
Because he was so strong.   [1782]

But the Eastern fires were stronger, they did not take
      Northland,
But became free of Dolojo.

We went to White River to be further from them
But they follow everywhere & we made war on them
Till they sent Black Snake, Genl. Wayne
Who made strong war.   [1792]

We made peace & settled limits and our next king was good and
        peaceful,
Hahking-pomskan, Hard Walker, who would not join
Our Brothers Shawanis & Ottowas nor Dolojo
In the new war.   [1811–12]

After the last peace come in crowds all around us the Yankwis,
They want again our lands of Wapahani, of Ohio;
It was useless to resist, for they are ever getting stronger
By increasing their United Fires.

Kithtilhund & Lapanabi were the chiefs of our two tribes
When we resolved to exchange our lands
And return at last beyond the Mississippi
Near our ancient Seat.

We shall be near our enemies the Osages
But they are better than the English Snakers
Who want to own the whole Big Island.
Shall we be free and happy there?

At the New Wapahani
we want rest
and peace
and wisdom

57

June 22, 1820. White River, Indiana.
Stopped here at Indian Village—4 wigwams by a bend.
Everyone but the old chief near death from variola. I have never
witnessed such a wretched scene—children, from infant babes
to about 9 yrs. wasted by fever, pocked with running pustules,
lying in swarms of flies within the foetid wigwams, odour
unbearable of foeces, rancid sweat and pus; some dozen adults
also low. All malnourished, no food left. None well enough
to gather berries or hunt a rabbit. Only the chief, with his face
scarred and pocked, immune from the infection. These are the
Delawares, or Lenni-Lenapes, forced, so the old man told me,
to remove here some years hence from the Penna. Mtns. Three
other villages nearby, all decimated by the smallpox. The rest
have moved on to the Western Territory. Fortunately I had
considerable morphine in my bag, which I doled out among
them; took the children out of doors—the day being mild—and
applied compresses of cold water; burned their bedding, set them
down on couches of fresh boughs, though in truth I hold little
hope for several. On the riverbank, a species of vine like clematis
with purple star-shaped flower and in the meadow, a variety of
dogbane new to me. These I plucked, and took the roots, and
pressed within my Bible, for Professor Rafinesque's collection.

July 9th. Returning, stopped again at Indian Town. And as I
feared, found all the children dead. Also five adults. Of this
village of two dozen souls now only half remain. Two entire
familys—one the old chief's son's—gone; the rest recover slowly,
thin as twigs. I doubt they can survive the next winter.

As we were packing up to leave the chief approached, a bundle in his arms. He set this down and with some ceremony said to me these words:

In consideration of my care for his people when Death had marked them and I came forth to save the few who have escaped the long dark sleep for another year, he would give me this, their Walam-Olum, a sort of Bible they have written in pictures upon maple shingles for their medicine men to gaze on and recall the history of their tribe. Now, he said, the tribe will no more wander; now that his son has joined his ancestors there's none to read the pictures and remember who they are. Now they are so few their history is over. Now, he said, the white man will have to keep in mind all that has happened to his people. He is the last, he said, of the sachems. There is no one left now to sing the Walamolum.

He is grateful, they are grateful, for my helping them, and as they know me to be a man of kindness and good heart he leaves with me their sacred writings.

I tried remonstrance with the poor old broken man—these bits of wood with scrawlings I make nothing of must mean much to his tribe, though meaningless to me. But he was gone, a sad shadow fading between the trees. If these cartoons in ochre scratched on wooden sheaves have any worth, Professor Rafinesque, whose mind is taken by all curious things, would know. I shall give the bundle to the Professor when, in Lexington, I deliver the botanicals and, while I tell him of my travels, we shall dine and split a bottle of wine together.

58

INSTRUCTIONS TO A PAINTER OF
WAGGONS AND TAVERN-SIGNS, 1835

What though the Meeting be dismayed
To see a painter ply his trade
With pictures graven,
It will not seem vain to Heaven
That here an honest living's made—

Thy alphabets spell liveries' fame,
Thy images, a tavern's name
For the unlettered.
No brush in all Bucks County's bettered
Thy works, so thou needst feel no shame.

Now let the Spirit bless thy sight,
Thy mind and hand move by its might:
Prophet Isaiah
Incite thee with his ancient prayer
Of Peace that cometh with the Light.

Recall how, when a boy, thou found
Solace, Care, and Love surround
Thee with their shining
At the farm of David Twining.
There the oxen pawed the ground,

There the fatling and the calf
Lowed and nuzzled in the chaff.
With bow and quiver
The Lenapes' last lone survivor
There trod the untamed woodland path,

There are forest creatures wild
With beasts of burden reconciled:
There ox and lion
Together eat the straw of Zion,
And leading them, a little Child,

And near, to salve the savage breast,
As in the Boydell print of West
Great Penn extends
His hand, that settlers be the friends
Of Indians, and their peace be blessed.

These images, in dreams enmeshed,
Shall by thy hand and brush be fleshed
Till art of thine
Conceives and hangs in Heaven this sign
Of the Inn where men's souls are refreshed:

59

The lion with the fatling on did move.
A little child was leading them in love,

The leopard with the harmless kid laid down.
And not one savage beast was seen to frown.

When the great PENN his famous treaty made
With indian chiefs beneath the Elm tree's shade.

The wolf did with the lambkin dwell in peace,
His grim carniv'rous nature there did cease,

163

60

TO THE MAKER OF 'A PEACEABLE KINGDOM'

You, or thee, as thou preferred to be addressed, were never
free of them again: the sleek musculature of tawny longtailed
jungle cats uncoiling in the foreground of your mind,
wolf and lambkin, bear and stolid ox as well, but why
in that block-jawed portrait by your cousin Tom (who won
what fame is his with a beardless image of young Abe
before he freed the slaves) does the square-muzzled lion
in his painting of you at your painting look so much like you?
So writhed the menagerie of your mind, wrestling
with that Great Schism among the Friends—

       whether the Soul is saved
       by inwardly
       pursuing virtue

       withdrawing from
       the world because
       the world rejects

       the Seed of Light—
       How can Quaker
       ploughshares tax the soil

       to pay for guns, for troops
       to set the torch
       to Indian villages?

       The Friends step down
       from the Assembly, so
       to harrow

individual
virtue, from
the world apart.

They read their Bibles
by their guttering
light, until

they have got
the Parables
by heart or rote.

     —Or should they seek the Light
        within the soul
    kindled, rekindled from
        that sacred coal
    of God's Altar that George Fox
        and William Penn
    and the Quaker martyrs
        centuries ago
    were warmed by, as your cousin
        Elias,
    Whitman's father's friend
        on Long Island preached,
    and in whose stead
        you testified
    in Pennsylvania with such
        recriminations
    on First days of men
        as good and firm
    in their belief
        as thee in thine?

—Wrenched with sorrow, it is then thy mind dwells
upon the Child, in infant frock disposed among
the creatures as in Richard Westall's illustration

in the Bible: the gift of circumstance
to the need your art—that of a copyist, you thought—required.
Your gift was what you made of what you copied: it was you
or thee, as thee would rather, alone who traced
Penn's Treaty with the Indians beside the Christ Child
to say that peace is possible in thy own soul
with his ship the *Welcome* on the homely Delaware
behind the Shackamaxon Elm. See, placid ripples
glimmer beneath the mountains of the Water Gap
with Child, leopard, fatlings, lions, calves
disporting on a foreground mound. Sixty times
that we know of, you laboriously made
—all its details different in each rendering—
this dream your patient hand enacted into forms,
shapes, colors, a frieze
that still your mind sees all afresh as though
the scene had never yet been painted, and must be.
Here, one time among those many, every figure
found the place in the design you didn't know
was that which best fulfilled its purpose,
the place your hand was seeking: the Child's hand
holding the Branch of Jesse, which is the vine, extending
like Penn's hand, his to the sachems but the Child's
poised with the Branch from which the Blood of Jesse flows
in the sky above the vessel, while on shore
tame and savage creatures of this world
balance each other in imperfect
symmetry of twinned fulfillments, Heavenly
figures close at hand and large, the mortals
very small and far away. The land
is wilderness gentled to pastoral
without a dwelling, house or barn intruding
upon the pureness of its possibility.

This, beneath a mild, inviting sky
you have bequeathed us. It was well
no patron sent you from your craftsman's shop
in Newtown with your paintpots of flat colors
to the Royal Academy for pagan tutelage;
left among your simple people with your gifts,
your deep self-doubts and your one Book,
you've given us this scene, framed
between the couplets you made rhymes of
from Isaiah's verses, filling the corners
with square medallions of the Dove descending
between the words—'Meekness' 'Innocence'
'Liberty'—spoken by the ancients
and ourselves in tongues:

       The phrases heard are praises
       of the Lord and Manito

       before the Spirit
       withdrew and the Light clouded—

       O could our life be blessed
       as it seemed to the Founder!

       What though his bequest, his quest
       quicken, then founder;

       what though our history lunge
       against Time's prison,

       in the lovely simplicity
       of your intricate icon

       we see how the soul, though bound
       in the body's cell

uses nerves, bones, brain,
musculature of the living

man in strife
with his imperfections

till from woe, from pain
—yours—may come

a completed image,
a Peaceable Kingdom

of Brotherly Love, as Penn
from his sufferings

conceived, from his own being
convinced that the Light

of that of God shines now
as ever it shone

in this commonwealth
of our birth

where the first red breath
the child draws

howls, because necessity,
necessity

thrusts us down
to earth, to earth.

61

. . . On City Hall, above our lights,
Penn's statue spreads indulgent arms,
still beckoning the Welsh, the Mennonites
toward his green outlying farms,

his head in the clouds, his mood
benign, though slum-blocks sprawl,
splotches of rot, across Penn's Wood.
Beyond, bulldozers snarl

as behind his back, high-rise
investments abruptly obtrude
on our only noble boulevard
proportioned to delight men's eyes.

We cram the days, put time to use—
no hour but is a rush hour, and where rushing?
Our history grows longer, longer.
It's life that's getting away from us

as the city changes, seethes with being.
Our Founder's feet are stuck
to the cranium of a clock
whose four faces gaze on us unseeing,

yet there's a spirit in this place
that sifts through hands that clasp
what only time can grasp
—Here possibilities of grace

like fragrance from rich compost cling
to leaves where our each deed
and misdeed fall. The Seed
stirs, even now is quickening.

ACKNOWLEDGMENTS

Much of the reading on which this poem is
based was undertaken with the aid of a
Fellowship for Independent Study and Research
from the National Endowment for the
Humanities in 1975–76. My thanks, for helpful
comments on my version of the *Walam Olum*,
to Dell H. Hymes; for reading an early draft of
'Treating with Indians' and saving me from
various errors, to Philip Booth, J. William Frost,
and John M. Moore; for reading the completed
work, to Anthony Hecht, Frederick Morgan, and
William Zaranka. My most abiding debt,
for encouragement over many years,
is indicated on the dedication page.

   For assistance and many courtesies I am
grateful to the staffs of the Friends Historical
Society Library, Swarthmore College; Friends
House Library, London; the Historical Society
of Pennsylvania; the Library of Congress;
the Pennsylvania Academy of the Fine Arts;
University Museum and the Van Pelt Library of
the University of Pennsylvania; and William C.
Baldwin, West Chester, Pennsylvania.

D. H.

Quotations from Penn's writings are based on *A Collection of the Works of William Penn*, edited by J. Sowle (London, 1726). I have drawn on many biographies of Penn, particularly those by Samuel H. Janney (*The Life of William Penn*, 3d ed., 1871), M. R. Brailsford, Catherine Owens Peare, and Arthur Pound. For the history and culture of the Lenni Lenape (Delawares) I have consulted the work of three generations of anthropologists at the University of Pennsylvania: Daniel G. Brinton, *The Lenape and Their Legends* (1881); Frank G. Speck in several works of which I have used principally *The Delaware Indian Big House Ceremony* (1931); and Anthony F. C. Wallace, *Teedyuscung: King of the Delawares* (1948). A further source is C. F. Weslager, *The Delaware Indians: A History* (1972).

    6-7)   A photostatic copy of Rafinesque's manuscript notebook is preserved in the University of Pennsylvania Museum. This contains his drawings of the glyphs; the Indian words they served to suggest to the shaman; and his crude translation of the *Walam Olum*, which he derived from the dictionaries of the Lenape language compiled by eighteenth-century Moravian missionaries. I have tried to give the verses metrical form and to bring into the translation elements of meaning that appear in the glyphs but not in the received Lenape text. My version is based on the text, interpretations of the glyphs, and the historical background given in C.F. Voeglin *et al.*, *Walam Olum or Red Score: The Migration Legend of the Lenni Lenape or Delaware Indians . . .* (Indianapolis: Indiana Historical Society, 1954).

    9)   'Penn's letter to the Chief Sachem . . .' Two letters are conflated here: William Penn to the Indian chiefs, dated 21 June and 21:2d month, 1682.

    12-20 and 26)   Penn, *A Letter . . . to the Committee of the Free Society of Traders . . . With an Account of the Natives, or Aborigines* (1683).

22) 'Penn's Treaty with the Indians' by Benjamin West: reproduced by permission of the Pennsylvania Academy of the Fine Arts.

23) I have drawn much information from Ellen Starr Brinton, 'Benjamin West's Painting of Penn's Treaty with the Indians,' *Bulletin of the Friends Historical Association* (1941), and from the files of the Pennsylvania Academy of the Fine Arts.

24) The treaty of 15 July 1682 is preserved in the collections of the Historical Society of Pennsylvania, by whose courtesy the signatures of the sachems are reproduced.

28) 'Calder's statue': The 37-foot statue of Penn, by the grandfather of the contemporary sculptor Alexander Calder, stands on the tower of Philadelphia's City Hall, 548 feet above street level. A municipal ordinance decrees this the highest structure in the city.

29) 'Let Pepys, Penn's rival . . .': *vide* Pepys, *Diary,* 21 October 1667.

30) 'Seeing as yet no such thing . . .': Quoted in Janney's *Life of Penn,* p. 31.

31) Carrickfergus: The British garrison of this fortress near Belfast mutinied in 1666. Penn, then twenty-one, aided the Earl of Arran in quelling the uprising and, as a reward for his distinguished service, was offered command of the troops at Kinsale by the Duke of Ormonde, Lord Lieutenant of Ireland.

32) This portrait of Penn in armor, one of three surviving copies of a lost original by an unknown painter, is reproduced by permission of the Historical Society of Pennsylvania.

35) Penn, *Some Fruits of Solitude,* 507–516. The italicised lines are the opening words of Thomas Loe's sermon, reported by Janney, pp. 30–31.

36) Based on Joseph Besse, *A Collection of the Sufferings of the People Called Quakers* . . . (London, 1753), Vol. 1.

39) Anecdote of the sword from Janney, chapter iii.

40) 'Amyraut's *sagesse*': Penn studied with Moise Amyraut, the liberal Huguenot theologian, at Saumur, in 1663–64.

42) The indented passages in quotations ('by the Grace of God . . . ,' 'Whereas our Trustie and well beloved Subject . . . ,' and

'haveing regard to the memorie and meritts . . .') are from the Royal Charter of the Province of Pennsylvania (4 March 1682) as given in *Charter to William Penn, and Laws of the Province of Pennsylvania Passed Between the Years 1682 and 1700* (Harrisburg, 1879).

44)   *Ibid.,* 'The Great Law or the Body of Laws,' passim, especially chapters XVI, XXVI, XV, LXXIII, LXXVI. 'For they weakly err . . .': Penn, preface to 'The Frame of the Government,' p. 92.

45)   Penn, 'The Frame of the Government,' *ibid.*

46)   Francis Daniel Pastorius, *Circumstantial Geographical Description of Pennsylvania* (1700), translated from the German by Gertrude Selwyn Kimball, revised by M. D. Learned; reprinted by permission of Charles Scribner's Sons from *Narratives of Early Pennsylvania, West New Jersey and Delaware,* ed. A. C. Myers (1912).

47)   Derived from Speck and Weslager.

48)   Gabriel Thomas, *An Historical and Geographical Account of Pennsylvania and West-New-Jersey* (1698).

49)   Effect of fur trade on tribal economy: Wallace.

50)   Penn's shipboard letter to Thomas Lloyd and others, 1684, quoted in Robert Proud, *The History of Pennsylvania* (Philadelphia, 1797), I, 189–90. A plaque bearing these words is affixed to the east Market Street entrance to City Hall, Philadelphia.

51)   The tercets translate Voltaire's IIIe. *Lettre Philosophique;* the passage from 'I tell you . . .' to '. . . upon your breast' is from his entry, 'Quakers,' in *Dictionnaire Philosophique.*

52)   Based on Wallace, *Teedyuscung: King of the Delawares.*

53)   Treaty of 25 August 1737 as given in *Pennsylvania Archives* I, 541–43 (1852). Sachems' autographs from *Colonial Records of Pennsylvania,* I.

54)   Walking Purchase: described in Wallace. Canessetego's speech from *Minutes of the Provincial Council of Pennsylvania* IV, 579–80 (1851).'Brother Onas': Iroquois name for Penn.

55)   Proclamation of war against the Delawares: *Minutes of the Provincial Council,* VII, 88–90. Speech of Pachgantschilas to the Christian Indians of Gnaddenhutten (Bethlehem, Penna.): John Heckewelder, *History, Manners, and Customs of the Indian Nations Who Once Inhabited Pennsylvania and the Neighbouring States* (1818), repr. in *Publications of the Historical Society of Pennsylvania,* XII, 81 (1876).

56)   Rafinesque's Ms. records this addendum to the *Walam Olum*, text without pictoglyphs, giving the history of the Lenapes since the arrival of the whites.

57)   Dr. Ward of Kentucky: Of Dr. Ward no trace remains save Rafinesque's notation that it was from him that he received the *Walam Olum*; see Voegelin *et al.*, *Walam Olum or Red Score.*

58)   'At the farm of David Twining': Title of a pastoral painting by Edward Hicks, who was adopted by the Twining family of Newtown, Penna. They were responsible for Hicks's convincement to the Society of Friends.

59)   'A Peaceable Kingdom' by Edward Hicks is reproduced by permission of the Friends Historical Library of Swarthmore College.

60)   'Sixty times/that we know of . . .': 'Many different estimates have been made of the number of paintings he made using *A Peaceable Kingdom* as the subject, to-day we can place the number at about sixty.'—Andrew J. Crispo, Foreword to *Edward Hicks, A Gentle Spirit* ('catalogue of a Bicentennial exhibition of the work of Edward Hicks,' New York, Andrew Crispo Gallery, 1975).

ABOUT THE AUTHOR

DANIEL HOFFMAN has published six books of
poems before *Brotherly Love.* His first volume
won the Yale Series of Younger Poets Award,
and he has received poetry grants from the
National Institute of Arts and Letters and the
Ingram Merrill Foundation. He is author also of
several well-known critical studies (among them
Poe Poe Poe Poe Poe Poe Poe and *Form and Fable
in American Fiction*). He has served as Consultant
in Poetry of the Library of Congress, has taught
at Columbia and Swarthmore, and is Poet in
Residence at the University of Pennsylvania.